Isaac Blackford
The Indiana Blackstone

Photo Courtesy of Indiana Supreme Court.

by

W. W. THORNTON
of the Indiana Bar

Edited by Douglas Fivecoat

W.W. Thornton

Table of Contents

W.W. Thornton

Introduction

This book is part of a larger initiative by the Indiana Supreme Court to collect and distribute the court's own history. Our projects range from biographies of Indiana's judges, to scholarly symposia at Indiana law schools, to the recent restoration of the Supreme Court chambers to its original 1888 appearance. In all these efforts, we seek to encourage Hoosiers to understand and appreciate their own institutions.

It is altogether fitting that we begin our series on Supreme Court justices with Isaac Blackford. He was, of course, a leading figure in shaping Indiana's early judiciary, but he was also an important influence during the state's formative years while serving as a Territorial judge and as the first Speaker of the House. By editing and publishing his *Blackford Reports* of Indiana's earliest Supreme Court decisions, Judge Blackford, already firmly established within Indiana's legal circles, became well known to judges and lawyers beyond our borders. Courts in many other states, and indeed the United States Supreme Court, cited his cases and referenced his reports.

Reading about Blackford's life and accomplishments can teach twenty-first century Hoosiers much about Indiana's rich past, her courts, and her leading figures. I take great pleasure in introducing you to Judge Isaac Blackford, through the eyes and words of a man who knew his life well – Judge William Wheeler Thornton.

Randall T. Shepard

Randall T. Shepard
Chief Justice of Indiana

Editor's Note

W. Thornton wrote *Isaac Blackford: The Indiana Blackstone* in 1930 at the age of 79. Thornton was a prolific writer and a well-established legal presence in both Indianapolis and across the state; during his lifetime he practiced law at Logansport, Crawfordsville and Indianapolis, presided as a Marion County Superior Court judge, and was the librarian of the Indiana Supreme Court. Thornton died in 1932 just over a year after completing this biography of Blackford and the manuscript was never published. The manuscript was given to the Indiana State Library and found its way into their Manuscripts Division where it has remained, largely unread, to this day.

Isaac Blackford was a prominent and well-respected jurist and public figure in his day, however modern lawyers and historians often overlook him. Indiana Supreme Court Chief Justice Randall T. Shepard wanted to change that and, to that end, entrusted to me the project of transforming Thornton's typewritten manuscript into a modern format for publication. I have retained much of Thornton's original style although this often appears awkward to the modern reader. The words, spellings, and grammar presented here remain largely Thornton's. I have performed only minimal editing and formatting in order to maximize readability. The citations, footnotes, and parenthetical notes in the text are Thornton's actual references as well, although moved from their original in-text style to more traditional footnotes. Also, a few citations, specifically the genealogy references, were converted into appendixes because their extreme length hampered the flow of the text.

This work is meant as a tribute to both Judge Isaac Blackford and to Judge William Thornton. It is the Court's hope that through this publication, Judge Thornton's efforts to revitalize the memory of Judge Blackford and his legacy of life and work in the 1930s can be realized today, and that Isaac Blackford will once again be recognized and celebrated for his many contributions to Indiana's legal history.

Douglas Fivecoat
Editor

W.W. Thornton

Author Biography

W illiam Wheeler Thornton was born to John A. and Ellen B. Thornton on June 27, 1851 at their home near Logansport, Indiana. Thornton was raised in Logansport and attended Cass County district schools and Seminary High School. He continued his education at Old Smithson College, a Universalist institution in Cass County. In 1874, Thornton began his study of the law working under the supervision of his Uncle Henry C. Thornton. In 1875, Thornton left Logansport to attend law school at the University of Michigan. Following graduation, Thornton returned to Logansport to enter private practice. In 1880, Thornton was appointed a Marion County Deputy Prosecutor under Daniel Baldwin and served in this capacity until 1883.

Thornton left Marion County in 1883 to resume private practice, this time at Crawfordsville in Montgomery County. In 1889, Thornton returned to Indianapolis when he was appointed Librarian of the Indiana Supreme Court.

He worked for the court until 1893 when he returned to private practice in the capital. While practicing in Indianapolis, Thornton served as a lecturer at the Benjamin Harrison Law School (now Indiana University School of Law-Indianapolis) and was appointed to the Marion County Superior Court bench in 1914. Judge Thornton served as the Dean of the Benjamin Harrison Law School until his death in 1932.

Thornton married twice. In 1882, he married Mary Freytag, the daughter of Judge Robert Groves of Logansport. Following Mary's death, Thornton married Miss Irene Blackledge of Indianapolis in 1911.

During his life, Thornton was a prolific writer on legal issues and, as is demonstrated by this manuscript, a student of Indiana's legal history. Some of his many published works include The *Universal Encyclopedia* (1883) [a fourteen hundred page legal encyclopedia for which Thornton wrote over half of the entries], *Statutory Construction* (1887), *Indiana Practice Code, Annotated* (1889) [co-author], *Lost Wills* (1890), *Indiana Municipal Law* (1891), *Railroad Fences and Private Crossings* (1893), *Indiana Practice Forms for Civil Proceedings* (1893), *Gifts and Advancements* (1893), *Decedent's Estates* (1895), *Indiana Township Guide* (1898), and *Indiana Instruction to Juries* (1914).

William Thornton was a life-long Republican and a long-time member of the Indiana State Bar Association. He participated in local community groups, including the Century Club, the Contemporary Gentlemen's Literacy Club, and the Nature Study Club. Judge Thornton was an active member of the Freemasons joining the society in 1894. He served as the orator of the Adoniram Grand Lodge of Perfection from 1901 through 1929 and orator emeritus until his death in 1932. Thornton attained the rank of thirty-third degree Scottish Rite Mason in 1922 and held memberships in the Mystic Shrine and the Royal Arch. Judge Thornton died on January 21, 1932, at the age of eighty, after a long illness.

Chronology of Isaac Blackford's Life

1786 (Nov. 6)   Isaac Blackford is born at Bound Brook, New Jersey.

1802   Blackford attends Princeton College in New Jersey.

1806   Graduates from Princeton and reads law with General George
                McDonald of Middlebrook, N.J.

1807   Reads law with Judge Gabriel Ford of Morristown, N.J.

1810   Blackford is admitted to the New Jersey bar.

1811   Blackford leaves New Jersey and heads west.

1812   Blackford arrives in Dayton, Ohio but moves on to Brookville, Indiana.
                He gains admittance to the local bar but moves to Vevay, Indiana to
                serve as cashier to the Vevay Territorial Bank.

1813   Blackford resigns from the Vevay bank and moves to Salem,
                Indiana in Washington County where he is appointed the first Clerk
                and Reporter of the County. Later that year, Blackford is appointed the
                Clerk of the Territorial House of Representatives.

1815 (Sept. 14)   Blackford receives his commission as the Judge of the First Judicial
                Circuit and moves to Vincennes, Indiana. He resigns within a few
                months due to the position's low salary.

1816   Blackford wins election as a Territorial Representative for Knox County
                and is chosen Speaker of the House.

1817 (Sept. 10)   Governor Jennings appoints Blackford to the Indiana Supreme Court.

1820   Blackford marries Caroline McDonald, daughter of Gen. George
                McDonald (Blackford's first mentor).

1821 (May 30)	Caroline Blackford dies while giving birth to their son, George.
1823	Blackford reappointed to the Indiana Supreme Court.
1825	Blackford receives the Democratic nomination for Governor but is defeated by James Brown Ray.
1826	Blackford runs for a U.S. Senate seat on the Democratic ticket but is defeated by former Governor William Hendricks.
1830	Blackford publishes the first *Blackford Report*.
1834	Publishes the second *Blackford Report*.
1835 (circa)	Isaac and Caroline's son, George, dies of illness in Louisville, Kentucky.
1836	Publishes the third *Blackford Report*.
1840	Publishes the fourth *Blackford Report*.
1844	Publishes the fifth *Blackford Report*.
1845	Publishes the sixth *Blackford Report*.
1847	Publishes the seventh *Blackford Report*.
1850	Publishes the eighth *Blackford Report*.
1853 (Jan. 3)	Blackford leaves the Indiana Supreme Court after failing to win election to the court following the constitutional changes of 1851 that required popular elections for Supreme Court judges.
1855 (Mar. 3)	Blackford accepts a judicial appointment to the newly created U.S. Court of Claims in Washington D.C.
1859 (Dec. 31)	Isaac Blackford dies in Washington D.C.

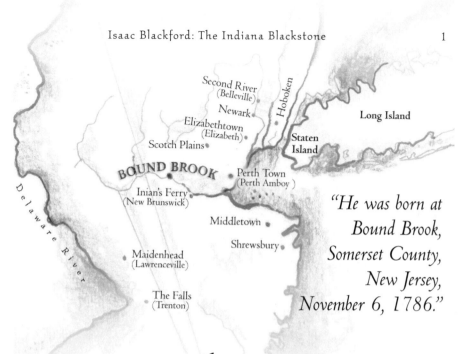

"He was born at Bound Brook, Somerset County, New Jersey, November 6, 1786."

Chapter I
Ancestors and Early Days

I saac Blackford, the Blackstone of Indiana, was of English descent, as his name indicates. He was born at Bound Brook, Somerset County, New Jersey, November 6, 1786. His father was a merchant of that place, who was born about 1757 and died May 22, 1800, when Isaac was only thirteen years of age. His name was Joseph Blackford. He was buried in the Presbyterian churchyard at Bound Brook, and on his tombstone is this singular verse:

Here lies the patron of his time;
Blackford expired in his prime,
Who three years short of forty-seven,
Was found full time and fit for heaven,
But for our loss weren't in my power,
I'd weep an everlasting shower.

It is an interesting thought, "Did Isaac have anything to do with writing the inscription?"

Who Isaac's grandfather was is a disputed question. One authority says he was Anthony Blackford; but another authority, it would seem, after a careful reading of the deed and will records of that county and vicinity, gives the opinion that it was Daniel Blackford, who kept a tannery, but later was a merchant, and who died August 21, 1814.[1]

Isaac's mother was Mary Staats Blackford. Her husband, Joseph's will of March 26, 1800, probated June 18, 1800 gave all of his property equally to his wife Mary (his sole executrix) and his son Isaac.[2] An inventory of January 7, 1801, shows personal property of $7,220.99, mostly in store goods and accounts owing. This will then showed that Isaac's mother was to take charge of Isaac as to clothing and education until he reached twenty-one, with this peculiar clause attached: "But in case my son proves disobedient to his mother and leaves her before he becomes of age aforesaid, then my said loving wife is no longer bound to pay for his bringing up as aforesaid; but, in case she thinks proper to pay, it must come out of his legacy."

It is quite evident Joseph left enough property to enable Isaac to secure a good education. Seven years after his father's death, Isaac invested $5,550 in a mortgage given him by one Thomas Coon on property in Bound Brook.[3]

Mary Staats Blackford resembled her son Isaac (or rather he resembled her) in personal appearance. She was of strong mind and full of the patriotism of 1776, and had great influence in molding his character. Her home was near one of the five battles in which Washington was the victor. Within her hearing were fought the battles of Trenton and Princeton; and she saw the British battalion fly to Kingston Bridge, and noted the ravages

---

[1] See Appendix One for Thornton's detailed discussion of Blackford's geneology.
[2] Trenton Wills Book 39, 46.
[3] This mortgage is unsatisfied of record. Was it never paid? His stepfather was the mortgagee.

of smallpox in the American Army. Amid the blasts of the winter of 1780-81 she carried food and clothing to the famished and ill clad patriotic soldiers who were camping near her door-yard. To such a mother a man usually traces his strongest excellences. Not later than 1801 she married Thomas Coon (the man to whom Isaac loaned his $5,550 and received a mortgage, on record in Somerset County). Coon was born about 1782, and died April 20, 1857. They had one child, Charlotte Teressa, born August 3, 1802. She inherited all of Isaac's estate on his death.

Mary Staats was probably the eldest daughter of Peter Staats, and was born on July 19, 1767. She died August 18, 1827.[4]

When Isaac Blackford's mother died he was "so deeply affected by the event that for six months he excluded himself from attendance upon court. To show how strong were his feelings and love for his mother, an intimate friend says he ever carried with him a lock of her hair, which was labeled 'my dear mother's hair', a memento of the object of his attention, and which recalled the cherished recollection of his childhood."[5]

Isaac Blackford, when he was sixteen years of age, was sent to Princeton College, and was registered as "Isaac Newton Blackford," a name he did not use in later life. (Perhaps the name "Newton" was inserted by mistake of the college registrar). His admission at the age of sixteen is testimony to the fact that in that time the standards for admission to our colleges were not very high. What was his training before

"Isaac Blackford, when he was sixteen years of age, was sent to Princeton College."

admission to the college we do not know, but we know generally that training in the ordinary common or popular schools of that day was not high.

The roster of the class he entered contains a membership of fifty-four.

---

[4] See Appendix Two for Thornton's citation about Charlotte Teressa and the Condit Genealogy.
[5] *Indianapolis Sentinel*, January 1860, editorial account of Blackford and his death.

The college had recovered from the effects of the Revolutionary War, when often classes had only half a dozen or so members.

Some of the members of his class afterwards attained high and honorable positions in civil life. There were John William Walker of Alabama, John James Marshall of Kentucky, Arnold Mandain of Delaware, Patrick Noble of North Carolina, Moulton 0. Rogers of Pennsylvania, Edward Colston of Virginia, Samuel Sprigg of Maryland, and James Iredell of North Carolina. Noble became Governor of North Carolina and a partner of John C. Calhoun; Sprigg became Governor of Maryland and a judge of the Supreme Court; Iredell, a son of Judge Iredell of the United States Supreme Court, became Governor of North Carolina, a judge of its Supreme Court, one of its United States Senators, and author of "A Treatise on the Laws of Executors and Administrators." Four of these named became judges of their respective states, three governors of them, and all were lawyers standing high in their profession. In addition to "A Treatise on Executors and Administrators," Iredell was the author of twenty-one volumes of the decisions of the Supreme Court of North Carolina, and Marshall of seven volumes of Kentucky.

Blackford excelled in Latin and Greek, attaining greater proficiency in these languages than is attained by the usual college graduate. He attained a position high up in the study of astronomy and higher mathematics, and in French. He was a great reader of the history of English customs and English history, a necessary study for a lawyer who desires to lay the foundations of his legal knowledge broad and deep. In college he acquired some knowledge of the Civil Law; and in his senior year read *Blackstone's Commentaries,* a work today regretfully neglected or even discarded. It is clear, from all that we know of him, he did not fritter away his time as so many college students now do.

He graduated in 1806, and then entered the law office of Colonel

George McDonald of Somerville, an eccentric, but able lawyer, whose office was then in Middlebrook, the hamlet of Revolutionary fame closely adjoining Bound Brook.[6]

Blackford remained in McDonald's office about a year, and then went into the office of Judge Gabriel Ford, of Morristown, then one of the most active practitioners of Morris County. Later, Ford became one of the justices of the Supreme Court of New Jersey.[7]

In these two offices his training was evidently excellent, if we may judge him in later years.

At the November term, 1810, he was admitted to the New Jersey bar. He was then twenty-four years old. It is evident he attained little practice in New Jersey. He was of such diffident demeanor that, as a young lawyer, we could not expect him to acquire a practice of much extent until mature years. An examination of the Court records of Morris and Somerset counties show scarcely an attempt to practice. Only one case shows his appearance in Court.[8]

From a business point of view, it would seem that Blackford should have remained in Morristown. Ford had a large practice when he went on the bench, and Blackford was thus afforded an opportunity to acquire some of it. As a student of retiring disposition and reared in a cultural atmosphere that offered inducements to stay in New Jersey near the vicinity of the

---

[6] For a sketch of Colonel McDonald, see *Somerset County Historical Quarterly* 5 (January 1916): 70. McDonald moved to Vincennes, Indiana, in 1819. He died in September, 1820, at the age of fifty-two and was there buried within a stone's throw of the resting place of Frances Vigo. Isaac Blackford's wife, Caroline, who died May 30, 1821, is buried near her father, Colonel McDonald. Samuel McDonald is also buried there. Judge Blackford erected to the memory of Colonel McDonald and his son, Samuel, two tombstones, one to each of them, on which are engraved his initials; and one to his wife having on it his initials, and this inscription: "Memory of Mrs. Caroline Blackford, consort of Isaac Blackford, who died May 30, 1821, in the 20th year of her age."

[7] His residence was in the house known then and now as "Washington's Headquarters".

[8] It was a case in the Common Pleas Court of Morris County, in 1811. Blackford one night in later years, had the privilege of occupying a room and bed that Washington and his wife had occupied. Several articles of furniture, even the carpet on the floor, were still in the room that had been there when Washington and his wife had occupied it.

scenes of his childhood, it is surprising that he left.

Evidently his mind was settled on going West. One source reports that he left New Jersey in 1811; and another, in 1812. The probability is he left late in 1811 and arrived in Dayton, Ohio in 1812 and this fact led to the confusion of dates. In one sketch of his life it is said, "unable to pay for a seat in a stage-coach, he walked to Clean Point on the Allegheny River, near the present site of Oil City, Pa., and from there floated down the river in a rude flatboat." The other is that he went west on horseback; so it is stated in one of the accounts of his entrance into Indiana.

He stopped at Dayton, Ohio, and then passed on to Lawrenceburg, Indiana, with letters of introduction to Isaac Dunn, where he began to prepare himself for practice in the Territorial Courts; but he did not remain there long, for in the same year of his arrival in the State, 1812, he went to Brookville.

Brookville, at the time, was sort of an eastern capital of the Territory. There, or shortly after, a number of distinguished men, or men who afterwards became so, were located. During 1812, he and Judge John Test went to Vincennes to secure a license for him to practice the profession of law.

Brookville was then only a village of two or three hundred inhabitants. The greater part of the State was yet in the grasp of the Indians. In November 1811, the battle of Tippecanoe had been fought, the most significant Indian battle up to that date, not only in Indiana but in the West. In September of that year, occurred the Pigeon Roost massacre, the bloodiest event for the number engaged that ever occurred in Indiana.

There were few roads in the State. Traveling was mostly on horseback, pushing new trails through the dense forests. Towns were scarce – often mere settlements in which lone emigrants lived. In many parts of the state, life, because of the Indians, was unsafe. There were no towns except in the southern third or fourth part of the Territory. There were no towns or settlements, no farms, in the remaining part, only two or three trading posts. Vast, magnificent forests covered the entire territory, except a stretch of prairie in the northwest part, which was practically unknown.

Into this vast wilderness, came Isaac Blackford in 1812. The contrast between his new and his old home – the rough pioneers and pioneer accommodations and practices, and the cultured people where he had been reared and had known, must have been very great. He must have had a stout heart to meet it or an unsatisfied condition in his eastern home to induce him to encounter it. There was some reason unknown to us for his coming West, unless it was the restlessness of the American to explore new fields or encounter new adventures. He believed there was a future in the West.

Blackford stood no chance of ever winning a living in the Circuit Courts of that day or any other day. Frankly, he was not "cut out" as a practicing lawyer for any day, as subsequent time demonstrated.

Within a few months after his admission to the bar he went to Vevay and became cashier of the Vevay branch of the Territorial Bank. While cashier he discovered that the bank officers were engaged in perpetrating a fraud upon the bank, and from this fact arose his aversion to and mistrust of banks that remained with him throughout his life.

In 1813 he moved to Salem, the county seat of Washington County, and was then, the same year, appointed the first Clerk and Recorder of the county. The same year in December, with the assistance of Isaac Dunn, he was appointed Clerk of the Territorial House of Representatives, then meeting in Corydon. That was the first meeting of the Legislature in the new Capital.

Corydon, at that time, was a town of only two hundred inhabitants, "a tiny bundle of log cabins in the midst of a sea of primeval forest." An Indianapolis newspaper thus describes it, its inhabitants and the surroundings: "in the lanes of Corydon, the adventurous sons of aristocratic

Virginia rubbed cloth elbows with the buckskin clad trappers, brown and silent as the Indian himself. The women wove the cloth for their clothing on their own spinning wheels. Land was plentiful, money was little needed. Business was a system of trade and barter. English shillings and Spanish dollars passed current; the merchant who made change chopped the silver coins into pieces and weighed each segment; justice was swift and salutary; lashes on the bare back were frequent; Judges held court on fallen logs in the midst of unbroken forests, and the sheriff had scalped Indians with his own hand."

Isaac Blackford became a familiar figure in the little communities of Corydon and Salem, but more often found his business led to old Vincennes, the capital of the Territory (1812). William Henry Harrison, then thirty-eight years old, was Governor of the infant territory; he was a Virginian, a graduate of Hampden-Sidney College, a son of a signer of the Declaration of Independence. In him, and in such men as Thomas Randolph of Virginia, the prosecuting attorney of Knox County (in which was Vincennes), the Judge of the General Court, Henry Vanderburgh,

"William Henry Harrison, then thirty-eight years old, was Governor of the infant territory."

Waller Taylor, Benjamin Parke, and the old Indian trader Colonel Francis Vigo, who had seen George Rogers Clark take Vincennes from the British thirty-three years before, Blackford found intellects which fired his ambition.

There was indeed, a score of lawyers in the Territory at that time (General Washington Johnston had been admitted to the Indiana bar in 1790, twenty-one years before), but the young Isaac Blackford was to surpass them all in his grasp of the law, and he it is who most justly may be called "the first lawyer of Indiana."[9]

---

[9] Quoted in *Somerset County Historical Quarterly* 5 (January 1916): 6. See Appendix One.

His chief duty as clerk at Salem was to record marks on cattle, which ran at large in the absence of stock enclosures. He served only one year as Clerk, when on September 14, 1815, then only twenty-nine years of age, he was appointed by Governor Posey judge of the First Judicial Circuit. Blackford then moved to Vincennes where he resided until he moved to Indianapolis. The First Circuit was composed of Knox, Gibson, Warrick, Posey, Perry, Pike and Daviess Counties. Benjamin Parke

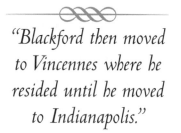

"Blackford then moved to Vincennes where he resided until he moved to Indianapolis."

was President Judge, having been elected by the General Assembly on December 21, 1816.

In Monk's *Courts and Lawyers of Indiana* an imaginary journey through the first circuit is given for Parke in 1817, which is just as applicable in 1815 to Blackford.[10]

We quote:

> Beginning his circuit at home at that time, he held court at Vincennes from the last Monday of February during the ensuing weeks. He then went to Princeton in time to open court on the second Monday of March. After two weeks session there, he proceeded through the wilderness along the trail to the Ohio [River]. His next court began at the county seat of Posey, at Blackford, a town named for Judge Blackford, and located at the northeast corner of what is the township. There, where cornfields now hold sway, the County of Posey had just completed, or perhaps the builders were still working on a magnificent courthouse. Twenty-six by twenty feet, to be built of logs of a handsome size, hewed down inside and out, one story and a half high, with one door fronting the street, and one window right opposite the door, with six panes of glass, eight by ten each; lower floor to be well laid with plank or puncheon, the upper floor to be

[10] Leander J. Monks, ed., *Courts and Lawyers of Indiana* (Indianapolis: Federal Pub. Co., 1916) 56.

laid with plank with a convenient staircase from the lower; the house to be well covered with a clapboard roof, with ribs and weight poles well pealed. One chimney to be handsomely built of sticks and mortar; the house to be well chinked and daubed, and also to be well underpinned; all the timber to be of good lasting quality; also one window to be cut in the gable end of the upper story finished as the window below; the house to be furnished with convenient shutters, all the other parts of said building to be finished and done in a workman like manner. [Such was the specifications for its construction.]

After a term of two weeks in this place of justice, the Judge had to make his way to Darlington, in Warrick, where another new courthouse had just been 'reared' at a cost of two hundred and ninety dollars. He opened court here on the fourth Monday of March (it may seem difficult to hold court at Blackford for two weeks after the third Monday of March and get to Darlington in time to open court the fourth Monday, but such was the law). This court calendar seems inexplicable, but as a matter of fact, the President Judge stayed for the important trials only and usually left the last week of the session in the hands of the Associate Judge.

Proceeding westward, our Judge had to traverse fifty miles of wilderness by the Evansville-Corydon post road, or perhaps by boat to Troy, the county seat of Perry, where, in the home of Associate Judge McDonald, he was due to hold court on the first Monday of April. Doubling on his trail after closing court at Troy, he headed north on the Maxville-Vincennes trail for Petersburg, where Pike's new county government was in operation on February 1, 1817.[11]

Allowing one week for each appointment, although the statute said two weeks, provided there was sufficient business, it would then require seven weeks, or approximately two months. The distance around the circuit was about one hundred and seventy-five miles, or twenty-five miles between appointments. The travel alone would require at least a full week.

---

[11] Of course, Blackford did not hold this court. His court here was to open on the second Monday of April and on the following Monday he was due at Liverpool (now Washington) Daviess County.

He was due for his second term of the year at Vincennes on the last of May, at Princeton on the second Monday of June; at Darlington, on the fourth Monday of June; at Troy, on the first Monday of July; at Petersburg, on the second Monday of July; at Washington, on the third Monday of July.

For his third trip, he started at Vincennes on the third Monday of September and opened his last court for the year at Washington on the third Monday of November. Thus for nine months of the year he was continually on the circuit. Courts were not in session at first during the winter months, but as new counties were formed and litigation increased, terms became longer and the whole year was consumed.

Blackford held his office for less than a year, when he resigned. The salary was only seven hundred dollars, but its purchasing power then was perhaps as much as two thousand dollars now.

In 1816, he was elected representative from Knox County to the House of Representatives. This was the first legislature elected after the state had been admitted to the Union. Delegates had been elected August 5, 1816, to the Territorial Legislature, which met at Corydon November 4, 1816 and continued to sit until January 3, 1819. The theory was that the Constitution of 1816 was in force on August 5th, having become so when the Constitutional Convention adjourned June 29, of that year, and the State's admission to the Union was not necessary to put it in force.[12]

Blackford was elected Speaker of the lower House. He was a popular man with the Representatives, notwithstanding there were a number of able men in the House. There is nothing to show he had any influence upon legislation – he may have had, but there is no record of it. In after

---

[12] Blackford served ten months as Circuit Judge and then resigned.

years, James Noble, who was elected United States Senator at this session of the Legislature, said of Blackford's career as Speaker: "His great fairness and unyielding integrity, to say nothing of his experience and natural fitness, won the respect and hearty goodwill of us all, and we could not find it in our hearts to oppose him."

John Johnson of Knox, James Scott of Clark, and Jesse L. Holman of Dearborn Counties, were nominated as Judges of the Supreme Court; and their nominations were affirmed by the State Senate. Their commissions bore the date of December 28, 1816.

During the May 1817 term of the Supreme Court, Judge Johnson died at Vincennes.

Governor Jennings, while walking arm in arm with Blackford from the grave of Johnson told him he had selected him from all the older and more experienced lawyers of the State to sit on the highest bench of the State in place of the deceased Judge. The announcement was entirely unexpected by Blackford. Jennings was a native of New Jersey, and that fact may have had something to do with his selection. Blackford begged hard not to receive such a mark of distinction, saying that he was too young in years for the position and lacked not only judicial experience but sufficient experience as a lawyer. But Jennings was obdurate and issued to him a commission dated September 10, 1817.

Blackford was then only thirty-one years of age. He continuously sat on the bench for thirty-five years — longer, probably, than any other judge in this country — not even Chief Justice Marshall who sat on the bench of the Federal Supreme Court at Washington for thirty–five years, exceeded the length of Blackford's service in a judicial career. Blackford sat until January 3, 1853.[13]

After his appointment as judge of the Supreme Court, Blackford continued to reside at Vincennes until at least 1830. It is not known at what date he moved to Indianapolis. He regarded Vincennes as his 'home' for

[13] As of June 2005, Blackford is still the longest serving judge of the Indiana Supreme Court.

"Governor Jennings, while walking arm in arm with Blackford from the grave of Johnson told him he had selected him from all the older and more experienced lawyers of the State to sit on the highest bench of the State in place of the deceased Judge."

Photo courtesy of Indiana State Library, Manuscripts Division.

Governor Jennings

many years after he came to Indianapolis.

Blackford, when he went upon the bench, was a very popular man — not the popularity of a man nominated for a purely political office, but that popularity that comes to a man in whom the people have the utmost confidence. Though a Democrat of moderate views, he was popular with the Whigs who looked upon him, not as a politician, but as a man of fairness, uprightness of character, of judicial learning, and whom they could trust and would not be betrayed. This is the finest popularity and that which is most prized.

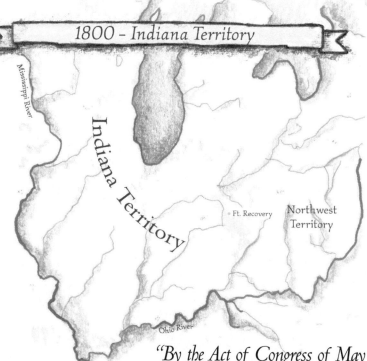

"*By the Act of Congress of May 7, 1800, the Northwest Territory was divided. The eastern part retained the name of the 'Northwest Territory' while the western part was called 'Indiana Territory'.*"

Chapter II
The General Court of the Territory and the Old Supreme Court

Since Blackford has now, in the course of our study of him, reached the Supreme Court of the State, it is well enough to stop and examine the history of both the Territorial General Court and the Old State Supreme Court, as it is usually called in distinguishing it from the Court created by the Constitution of 1851 and first the Territorial Court.

THE TERRITORIAL GENERAL COURT

By the Act of Congress of May 7, 1800, the Northwest Territory was divided. The eastern part retained the name of the "Northwest Territory," while the western part was called "Indiana Territory," with Vincennes as its capital, or the seat of government. The United States census of that year shows there were 45,365 inhabitants in the eastern part, and only 5,641 in the western part, or Indiana Territory.

The government of the Indiana Territory began July 4, 1800, when only John Gibson, Secretary of the Territorial officers, was on hand. William Clark, Henry Vanderburg and John Griffin had been appointed Territorial Judges, but they took no action until after the arrival of Governor Harrison, January 10, 1801. Until then Gibson was the whole government.

Immediately on his arrival, Harrison called a session of the Council of the Governor and Judges for January 12, 1801. They had legislative powers; and at this session, adopted six laws and three resolutions. All but one of these laws were amendatory or a repeal of certain laws of the Northwest Territory which were then held to be in force in the Indiana Territory.

Under the Ordinance of 1787 the Governor and Judges had power to "adopt and publish in the district such laws of the original states, criminal and civil" as might be necessary and best suited to the circumstances of the district and report them to Congress from time to time, which laws were to "remain in force in the district until the organization of the General Assembly therein, unless disapproved by Congress"; but afterwards the Legislature was given authority to alter them as they "might see fit."

While in the adoption of laws the court is an interesting study, we are more interested in the sessions of the court than we are in those of the Council of the Governor and Judges. Court was held at Vincennes March 3, 1801. Thus runs the official record of the proceedings: "At a General Court of the Indiana Territory, called and held at Ft. Vincennes the third day of March, in the year one thousand eight hundred and one, the commissions of the Judges of the General Court being read in open court, they took their seats, and approved William Clark, Henry Vanderburgh, and John

"At a General Court of the Indiana Territory, called and held at Ft. Vincennes the third day of March, in the year one thousand eight hundred and one..."

Griffin Judges. Henry Hurst, Clerk of the General Court, having produced his commission from the Governor and a certificate of his having taken the oath of allegiance and oath of office, took his place. John Rice Jones, Attorney General, produced his commission, and a certificate of his having taken the oath of allegiance and the oath of office."

Thus began the Territorial Court, which was really the first Supreme Court in Indiana. Its judges had general supervision over lower courts, "to examine and correct all manner of errors of the justices of the inferior courts in their judgments, processes and proceedings in the said courts, as well as in all pleas of the United States, as in all pleas real, personal and mixed, and also to examine, correct and punish the contempts, omissions and neglects, favors, and defaults of all or any of the Justices of the Peace, sheriffs, coroners, clerks, and other officers within said respective counties."

It is thus seen that the General Court was a court of both original and appellate jurisdiction. Appeals lay to it from Courts of Common Pleas and Circuit Courts; and writs of error could be issued by it to both of these courts, and also to justices of peace.

In its main features the practice in appeals was similar to that of today. As today, before a case could be taken to the Supreme Court it must have been prosecuted to a final judgment. The amount at issue must be at least fifty dollars in a civil suit or relate to a franchise or freehold. The appellant had to furnish a bond and an authenticated copy of the record below. If the appellant failed, he had to pay the appellee a sum not greater than ten percent of the amount of the judgment, by way of damages caused by delay.

In a number of instances, the Supreme Court delivered written opinions while sitting in its capacity as an appellate court, and they were entered at length in its order books, but none of them has ever been published.

The judges possessed the power to hold court in the circuit courts. In the exercise of this power, Judge Parke tried his first case in Wayne County, riding all the way from Vincennes for that purpose alone. He had a log for a desk. It was a case of theft of a twenty-five cent pocket knife.

The most important case that came before the Territorial Court was that of Governor Harrison against James McIntosh for slander. McIntosh was a Scotchman a near relative of Sir James McIntosh, the English philosopher and statesman, and perhaps the wealthiest man at Vincennes. From being a close friend of Harrison, he turned to be a bitter enemy, and charged him with having cheated the Indians. In the spring of 1811, Harrison sued him for slander. Vanderburgh and Parke declined to sit, the first because he was a personal friend of the defendant, and the other, because he was a strong personal friend of the plaintiff. This left Waller Taylor as the sole judge. Eleven were appointed to select the names of forty-eight citizens as a panel from which the jury was to be taken. From these the plaintiff and defendant each struck off twelve names, and from the remaining twenty-four the jury was selected by lot. This was practically our present method of securing a "struck jury."

Thomas Randolph appeared for Harrison, and Elias Glover and Gen. W. Johnston for McIntosh. The jury was impaneled April 10, 1811; and the trial held the same day, beginning at ten o'clock in the morning, and lasting until one o'clock a.m. the next day, April 11, when a verdict of four thousand dollars damages was returned, and judgment entered upon it at once against McIntosh. The jury was out only one hour. McIntosh's land was levied upon to satisfy the judgment, and the Governor's agent, while Harrison was in command of the army, bid it in. Afterwards Harrison returned two thirds of the land to McIntosh, and gave the remaining third to the orphan children of several distinguished citizens who fell in the War of 1812.

"The Court sat at Vincennes, until the Capital was removed to Corydon in 1813 under an Act of March 11 of that year, and there remained until superseded by the Supreme Court provided for by the Constitution of 1816."

Photo courtesy of Indiana State Library, Manuscripts Division.

Indiana's Early State Capitol (Corydon, Indiana)

The Court sat at Vincennes, until the Capital was removed to Corydon in 1813 under an Act of March 11 of that year, and there remained until superseded by the Supreme Court provided for by the Constitution of 1816. In Corydon, its sessions were probably held in the Court House in the large upper room when the Legislature was not in session.

THE OLD SUPREME COURT

It is the Old Supreme Court, as it is now called to distinguish it from the present Supreme Court, in which we are most interested.

By an Act of April 19, 1816, the inhabitants of the Territory of Indiana were authorized to form for themselves a constitution and State government, and to assume such name "as they deemed proper."

The population, taken pursuant to an Act of the Territorial Legislature, was 63,897 distributed throughout the thirteen counties that then occupied the entire State.

Congress had named May 13, 1816, as the day on which delegates to the Constitutional Convention should be chosen, and the tenth of the next month for their assemblage at the Territorial Capital. They held their session in the Court House at Corydon, but when the weather was excessively warm, they held them under a large elm tree a square away, long known, until it decayed and was removed, as the "Constitutional Elm."

The Convention finished its labors in twenty days. It consisted of forty-three delegates. On December 11, 1816, by joint resolution, Congress resolved, "that the State of Indiana should be one, and is hereby declared to be one, of the United States of America and admitted into the Union on an equal footing with the original States, in all respects whatever." Section Two of Article Four of the new constitution declared:

> The Supreme Court shall consist of three judges, any two of whom shall form a quorum, and shall have appellate

jurisdiction only, which shall be coextensive with the limits of the State, and such restrictions and regulations, not repugnant to this constitution, as may from time to time be prescribed by law. Provided, nothing in this article shall be so construed as to prevent the General Assembly from giving the Supreme Court original jurisdiction in capital cases, and cases in chancery, where the president of the circuit court may be interested or prejudiced.

Section Four of Article Five provided:

The judges of the Supreme Court, the circuit, and other inferior courts, shall hold their offices during the term of seven years, if they shall so long behave well, and shall, at stated times, receive for their services, a compensation which shall not be diminished during their continuance in office.

Section Seven of the same Article declared:

The judges of the Supreme Court shall be appointed by the Governor, by and with the advice and consent of the Senate. The presidents of the circuit courts shall be appointed by joint ballot of both branches of the General Assembly; and the associate judge of the circuit courts shall be elected by the qualified electors in the respective counties.

Section Eight of the same Article declared:

"The Supreme Court shall appoint its own clerk."

And Section Ten says:

When any vacancies happen in any of the courts, occasioned by death, resignation, or removal from office, of any judge of the supreme or circuit courts, or any of the clerks of said courts, a successor shall be appointed in the same manner as heretofore prescribed, who shall hold his office for the period which his predecessor had to serve, and no longer, unless reappointed.

The question of the adoption of the Constitution as passed by the delegates was not submitted to a vote of the people. It was considered that its passing and adoption by the convention delegates put it in force, and they so declared. Before the State was admitted into the Union, the state legislature met on the first Monday in November, the fourth, 1816 at Corydon, and adopted an Act for the organization of the Supreme Court, which was approved. December 26, 1816, and which took effect on the first day of the following February.

"Duels were then common, even among public men."

Duels were then common, even among public men. Andrew Jackson ten years before had fought three duels, and in the last one deliberately killed his opponent after his opponent had emptied his pistol by firing first at him. And that was after he had been Judge of the Supreme Court of Tennessee. So the Legislature adopted the following oath for all judges and other government officials to take, which was afterwards carried into the *Revised Statutes* of 1824 as an addition to the oath of allegiance:

> All officers in and belonging to the legislative department of government, who are now, or shall be hereafter elected, before they enter upon the discharge of the duties of the aforesaid offices, shall take the following oath in addition to what is now by law directed to be administered to them, that 'he or they (as the case may be) have neither directly nor indirectly given, accepted or knowingly carried a challenge to any person or persons to fight in single combat, or otherwise with any deadly weapon, either in or out of this state since the twenty-ninth day of June, 1816; and that he or they, will neither directly or indirectly, give, accept or knowingly carry a challenge to any person or persons, to fight in single combat or otherwise, with any deadly weapon either in or out of this state during their continuance in office; and upon their refusing to take the oath aforesaid, their office shall be vacate, and be filled in the same manner as if they had resigned.'

The Act for the organization of the Supreme Court provided for two terms a year – one commencing on the first Monday in May, and the other on the corresponding day in December (in 1820, a change was made from

December to November). The Court was authorized to sit in the County Court House at Corydon. Each term was thirty days, if the business before the Court required a term of that length of time; but the court was given power to extend the term indefinitely.

The business then pending in the General Court of the Indiana Territory was transferred to the Supreme Court, except such cases as were originally brought and then pending in the courts at Vincennes and Brookville, which were sent to the Circuit Courts sitting at those two places. Any case brought in the court at Corydon could be sent, by order of the court, to the county where it originated, or where one of the parties resided. All appeals cases were retained.

The first session of the state legislature increased the number of the counties to seventeen. There were three judicial circuits. The first contained the counties of Knox, Gibson, Warrick, Posey, Perry, Pike and Daviess. The second, Harrison, Clark, Washington, Jackson and Orange; and the third, Wayne, Franklin, Dearborn, Switzerland and Jefferson. The boundaries of these counties were very different from those bearing the same names at the present day, or even when the Constitution of 1851 was adopted.

Travel was almost impossible, and rivers and creeks were often unfordable. The steamboat had not yet appeared in western waters, and in fact was yet practically an experiment. The raft, the dugout, and the pirogue were the only means of navigation.

"The first session of the State Legislature increased the number of the counties to seventeen. There were three judicial circuits."

Settlements were far apart. The Indians still lived within the State in goodly numbers. As we have elsewhere stated, the population was 63,897. In December, 1815, Wayne County had only 6,407 souls; Franklin 7,370; Dearborn, 4,424; Jefferson, 4,270; Washington, 7,317; Harrison, 6,975; Gibson, 5,330; Knox, 8,066; Switzerland, 1,832; Clark, 7,150; Posey,

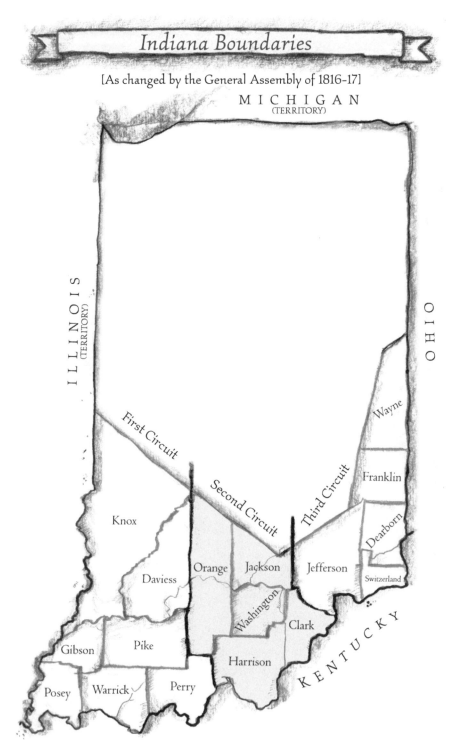

Indiana Boundaries

[As changed by the General Assembly of 1816-17]

MICHIGAN
(TERRITORY)

ILLINOIS
(TERRITORY)

OHIO

KENTUCKY

First Circuit

Second Circuit

Third Circuit

Wayne

Franklin

Dearborn

Knox

Orange

Jackson

Jefferson

Switzerland

Daviess

Washington

Clark

Gibson

Pike

Harrison

Posey

Warrick

Perry

1,619; Perry, 1,720; and Warrick, 1,415. Brookville had been laid out only five years, and had only eighty houses, "exclusive of shops, stables, and outhouses." Salisbury (now entirely disappeared) was the county seat of Wayne County, and had "about thirty-four houses, two stores, and two taverns"; and already Centerville (afterwards the county seat) was rivaling it. Vevay had been laid out only three years, and had eighty-four dwellings, besides thirty-four mechanic's shops, a brick courthouse, brick jail, brick schoolhouse, brick markethouse, brick church, eight stores, three taverns, two physicians, a library of three hundred volumes, a "literary society," in which "were several persons of genius, science and literary," and two lawyers. Madison had sixty or seventy dwellings, and a bank. Jeffersonville had one hundred and thirty houses, a post office, and a land office (it was laid out in 1811). Clarksville, just below it had only forty houses, "most of them old and decayed." New Albany, says an old chronicle, "a short distance below Clarksville, has been puffed throughout the Union, but has not yet realized the anticipations of its proprietors." Corydon had been a town only seven years, but had a stone courthouse; and Paoli was just settled. Vincennes had a hundred houses, a population of about 1,000; and Terre Haute had just been laid out. Lawrenceburg had about three hundred inhabitants, but was considered a town of much importance. Rising Sun had less than one hundred houses, North Lexington, fifty; Charlestown, one hundred and sixty, "chiefly of brick, a handsome courthouse;" and Salem, eighty. The cities of Indianapolis, Crawfordsville, Frankfort, Lafayette, Logansport, Peru, Wabash, Huntington, Elkhart, South Bend, Kokomo, Anderson, Muncie, Richmond, Greenfield, Noblesville, Lebanon, Danville, Franklin, Martinsville, Tipton, Shelbyville and Rockville were unknown and undreamed of, and even Fort Wayne was only a trading post.

There was little wealth and land was too cheap to seriously engage one in a legal contest for its possession. How many lawyers there were within the

State it is impossible to state: but we have seen Vevay had only two. Knox, being the oldest and wealthiest county, had more attorneys than any other county; but even here, if we may judge of the number as shown by its records, admitted by the General Court of the Territory to practice law, they were scarcely more than a dozen in number. In the entire State there were far below one hundred in number.

"The lawyers of that day," it is said in *Courts and Lawyers of Indiana*, regarding 1816:

> Were by far the best-educated class of men in that early society. The struggle which they carried on successfully with the powers of crime and confusion required not only professional skill and physical courage, but it also required the vision of seers who could see in that wild society the possibilities of great States. It required skill and patience to discern the good and the evil, discrimination to separate them and, while driving out the vicious, to nurture carefully the forces of progress.[14]

Governor Jennings appointed James Scott, John Johnson, and Jesse L. Holman judges of the Supreme Court, and their appointments were approved by the State Senate. Their commissions bore the date of December 28, 1816.

"On the 5th day of May, 1817, the day appointed by law for the commencement of the first term of the Supreme Court," says Blackford in his first entry in his first volume of reports, "the judges appeared and took their seats." This took place in the Court House in Corydon. Henry Hurst, clerk of the old Territorial General Court, and afterwards of the United States District Court, at Indianapolis, was the first clerk. The Sheriff of Harrison County, of which Corydon was the county seat, served as Sheriff of this Court.

In 1817, "the political affairs of the State," says Oliver H. Smith, "were

---

[14] Monks, *Courts and Lawyers of Indiana*, 19.

in the hands of three parties, or rather one party with three divisions – the Noble, Jennings, and Hendricks divisions – which were all represented in the Convention that formed the Constitution of 1816. It was evident to these leaders that personal political conflicts must arise between them unless the proper arrangements were made to avoid them. It was thus agreed among them to aid each other in making Noble a United States Senator, Jennings the Governor, and Hendricks a Congressman. Each division was entitled to one selection to the court. Gen. Noble selected Jesse L. Holman, living on the beautiful heights of the Ohio River, above Aurora, a good lawyer and one of the most just and conscientious men I ever knew. Gov. Jennings selected John Johnson, a fine lawyer and an excellent man. Hendricks, named James Scott of Clark County, a Pennsylvania man, one of the purest men in the State, a good scholar, and a fine lawyer."[15]

During the court's first vacation Judge Johnson died at his residence in Knox County, "universally esteemed," says Blackford, "as an honest man, and as an independent, intelligent man." Isaac Blackford was appointed his successor September 10, 1817 and took his seat on the first day of the December term of that year.

Scott, Holman, and Blackford at the end of their first term were reappointed, and continued to serve until the end of their terms, December 28, 1830.

Governor Ray, for some reason that cannot be satisfactorily determined, resolved to break up the Old Supreme Court when they had finished their second terms. On January 28, 1831 Ray appointed, Gen. John T. McKinney of

"Governor Ray, for some reason that cannot be satisfactorily determined, resolved to break up the Old Supreme Court, when they had finished their second terms."

[15] Oliver Smith Hampton, *Early Indiana Trials and Sketches* (Cincinnati: Moore, Wilstach, Keys & Co., 1858) 84.

Franklin County, Stephen C. Stevens of Jefferson, and reappointed Blackford January 28, 1831. The refusal of Governor Ray to reappoint Scott and Holman was charged at the time and generally believed, because they had refused to support him in his candidacy for the United States Senate. He and Blackford had been opposing candidates for governor in 1825 when he defeated Blackford; and he no doubt thought he could make friends in the Blackford ranks by reappointing him. In this he was grievously disappointed; for Blackford was no politician. The action of Ray in refusing to reappoint the full bench rendered him very unpopular.[16]

Judge Stevens resigned in 1836 and Charles Dewey was appointed May 30, 1836 to fill the vacancy caused by Stevens' resignation. Judge John T. McKinney died at his residence in Brookville, May 29, 1837. Jeremiah Sullivan was appointed his successor on May 29, 1837 and took his seat at the May term, 1837.

Blackford was reappointed January 19, 1845, for seven years, from January 28, 1845, and served until January 3, 1853, when the Old Supreme Court came to an end by reason of the change of the government under the Constitution of 1851.

The terms of the office of the judges of the Supreme Court expired in 1846. Whitcomb was elected Governor in 1847 and served until 1849. He was a Democrat. The Democrats were in the saddle; and their slogan was, "Turn out the rascal Whigs, who have been in office too long. Some 'pie' must now be put on the counter." The example of Governor Ray may have had some influence. The great majority of the people expected to see the old judges reappointed. But Governor Whitcomb refused to reappoint them; for what reason it has never been satisfactorily determined. On one occasion, however, he said they were too old and there was need of young men to clear the docket then far behind.

He first appointed Charles H. Test and Andrew Davison; but the Senate

---

[16] Monks, *Courts and Lawyers of Indiana*, 194.

failed to confirm them. He then nominated E. M. Chamberlain and Samuel E. Perkins. These were rejected. Then followed the nomination of W. W. Wick and James Morrison who were also rejected. When these were rejected he appointed Samuel E. Perkins and Thomas Smith to serve until their successors were confirmed by the Senate.

It appears the Old Court was sacrificed on the altar of politics; for Dewey and Sullivan were Whigs, and Blackford was a Democrat. There was no trouble over Blackford's confirmation; and probably would not have been over Dewey and Sullivan if they had been Democrats.

Perkins was temporarily appointed January 21, 1846, in place of Sullivan, to continue until the end of the next session of the Legislature, and January 29, 1847, he was reappointed for seven years from this last date.

Thomas L. Smith was likewise appointed on the same date, to serve for like terms.

Under the constitution of 1851 the judges were selected by popular vote. Indiana, by Act of February 19, 1852, was divided into four districts, and one judge was elected from each district. None of the judges except Perkins of the Old Court, were nominated as judges under the new constitution. Blackford and Perkins were competitors for the nomination, and Perkins, being the better politician, was nominated and elected. The new judges were Samuel E. Perkins, Andrew Davison, William Z. Stuart and Addison L. Roache. They were elected October 12th, 1852.

The statute for the organization of the New Court provides that it should convene on the first Monday in January, 1853, in the old house (usually called "the Governor's Mansion") in the Circle in Indianapolis, and draw up such rules as were necessary for its procedure.

The judges of the Old Court sat in five cases January 1, 1853, as shown in the fourth *Indiana Report*. Their terms expired January 3, 1853. The last case in which an opinion was filed was <u>Reynolds v. Rochester</u> (4 Ind. 43) and Perkins wrote the opinion. The clerks of the General Territorial Court were Daniel Lymmes, 1794-1808; Henry Hurst, 1804-1816; of the Old Supreme Court, Henry Hurst 1816-1820, Henry Coburn 1820-1852; and William Beach 1852, who continued as clerk of the New Supreme Court until 1860.

Some idea of the amount of work the Old Supreme Court judges performed may be drawn from the number of cases reported in the eight *Blackford* and first three *Indiana Reports*. These eleven volumes contain 2,333 opinions, and 500 cases disposed of by memoranda. Of these opinions Blackford wrote 845, Dewey 383, Perkins 271, Sullivan 253, Smith 209, Holman 138, Scott 97, Stevens 711 and McKinney 66. As Blackford was continuously on the bench for thirty-five years, he, of course, wrote more opinions than his fellow associates who each served fewer years.

These reports, however, do not show the extent of the judges' entire labor; for the dockets show many cases, usually dismissals that come before the court and which required attention. They did not attain the dignity of an opinion.

The Court continued to sit at Corydon until the capital was removed to Indianapolis under the Act of January 20, 1824. The General Assembly convened in Indianapolis January 10, 1825; and pursuant to the Act of 1824, the Supreme Court convened there May 2, 1825. The removal of the State offices required a journey of one hundred and twenty-five miles and was a difficult task. The roads, in many places were almost impassable, and the task of removal was a serious one.

Marion County was established by the Act of December 31, 1821. The site of Indianapolis had already been selected as the place of the new capital; and, with an eye to the future needs of the State the Legislature donated to the county $8,000 for a court house, suitable for a State House until one should be built, which was to be commenced when the Act of 1821 took effect; and to be completed within three years thereafter. It was erected on the square where the present courthouse of Marion County now (at the time of writing – 1930) stands.[17] It continued to be the meeting place of

[17] EDITORS NOTE: The Marion County Courthouse was demolished in 1962. It stood to the south of the current city-county building at Alabama and Washington Streets.

"It continued to be the meeting place of the Legislature until the old Capitol building was erected in 1835."

'Old' Capitol Building (Erected 1835) - *Indianapolis*

the Legislature until the old Capitol building was erected in 1835.

The old Court House was practically the only public building in the town from 1825 to 1835. The Legislature made a State House of it for three months every year. The Federal Court, the Supreme Court, and the County Board all met and did business there. More than this, after the completion of the State House (in 1835) and the removal of that portion of the public business to its own quarters, the old Court House became the City Hall, the place of conventions, the ready resort of every gathering that could not go any where else and could pay for lights there.[18]

The Supreme Court met in the old Court House when the General

---

[18] Berry R. Sulgrove, *History of Indianapolis and Marion County* (Philadelphia: N.P., 1884) 45.

Assembly was not in session and its clerk there had his office. But "in 1827 the Legislature appropriated five hundred dollars to build a double room, one story brick house at the west entrance of the Court House Square, for the clerk of the Supreme Court." "This building was torn down in 1855, and the clerk's office removed to the State House."[19]

A building that cuts some figure in the history of the Old Supreme Court was one known as the "Governor's Mansion." It stood in the center of the Circle, now known as "Monument Place"; and stood where the Indiana Soldiers and Sailors Monument now stands.

In 1827 the Legislature appropriated four thousand dollars for a mansion for the Governor in, as it was then called, "the Governor's Circle," which was ordered to be enclosed by a rail fence. Its completion cost $6,500. It was a large, square, brick building, about fifty feet each way, with two full stories. A hall ran through it north and south, and another at right angles east and west. It was six feet above the ground, with steps leading up to the hall doors. On the second floor were four rooms, but somewhat smaller than the lower ones. It was never used for a residence, and never occupied by a Governor. The Supreme Court judges had their chambers there. Blackford for many years made one of the rooms practically his home. The Legislature of 1856-57 ordered it sold. It was auctioned off April 16, 1857 and brought $665. It was used for nearly thirty years for most of the State office purposes, except the State treasury.[20]

By Act of 1832 the Supreme Court was authorized to adjourn from the Court House "to any other house in the town of Indianapolis;" and the judges were given the privilege of occupying one of the rooms in the Governor's Mansion "for a consultation room," either in term time or in vacation. The open sessions of the Supreme Court were held either in the consultation room or in a convenient room in the old Court House.

---

[19] Sulgrove, *History of Indianapolis*, 45-46.
[20] Sulgrove, *History of Indianapolis*, 59.

"A building that cuts some figure in the history of the Old Supreme Court was one known as the 'Governor's Mansion.' It stood in the center of the Circle, now known as 'Monument Place;' and stood where the Indiana Soldiers and Sailors Monument now stands."

"Governor's Mansion" on the Circle - *Indianapolis*

While not practically germane to the subject, yet we may note something of the attorneys who were members of the bar of the Supreme Court. Forty-eight attorneys appeared in the cases reported in the first *Blackford [Report]*.

Practicing in the Supreme Court at the commencement of the May Term, 1848, were the following, except those marked with an asterisk who had previously died:

*Amos Lane

J.R.E. Goodlet

Henry P. Thornton

Charles Dewey

Jeremiah Sullivan

Stephen C. Stevens

John H. Thompson

James Raridan

John Law

James Morrison

Amory Kinney

George H. Dunn

Michael G. Bright

Samuel Judah

Oliver H. Smith

William W. Wick

Hiram Brown

Albert S. White

Robert A. Chandler

William Herrod

Craven P. Hester

Charles H. Test

Henry Cooper

Andrew Ingram

James Farrington

David Wallace

Jesse D. Bright

Phillip L. Spooner

Samuel C. Willson

Ovid Butler

James Perry

Randall Crawford

Abner T. Ellis

Martin M. Ray

William N. Jenners

John Eccles

John Cowgill

*Nilliam Quarles

Benjamin Bull

Andrew Davison

Henry Chase

William J. Brown

Caleb B. Smith

John A. Brackenridge

John S. Newman

David Kilgore

Hugh L. Livingstone

David Macy

John Dumont

David H. Colerick

Rufus A. Lockwood

Joseph L. Jernegan

John Pettit

Richard W. Thompson

William P. Bryant

Courtland Cushing

R.N. Carnan

Stephen Major

John M. Johnston

Henry S. Lane

George G. Dunn

John B. Howe

Simon Yandes

Lewis P. Coppersmith

Hiram Allen

Daniel Mace

Elias S. Terry

John B. Niles

Abram A. Hammond

Robert S. Cox

Joseph A. Wright

John S. Watts

Robert C. Gregory

Williamson Wright

William H. Coombs

Zebulon Baird

David Brier

Lucian Barbour

Jeremiah Smith

Hugh O'Neal

Robert Brackenridge

John H. Bradley

John Brownlee

Thomas L. Sullivan

Walter March

Pleasant A. Hackleman

George B. Tingley

Jonathon A. Liston

Daniel Kelso

George Holland

Joseph G. Marshall

Samuel W. Parker

John W. Wright

Reuben D. Logan

Finley L. Maddox

Benjamin F. Gregory

Joseph E. McDonald

George B. Joiner

Andrew Ellison

William A. Porter

George Taylor

John G. Walpole

Isaac H. Klersted

Fabius M. Finch

John T. Morrison

Samuel A. Huff

William D. Griswold

John Yaryan

James A. Fay

*Robert M. Cooper

Martin Ray

Matthew S. Ward

Benjamin M. Thomas

William H. English

Jesse P. Siddell

Edward H. Brackett

David Linton

William T. Otto

*Alanson J. Stephens

James B. Sleith

Robert Jones

John P. Usher

Edward W. McGaughey

Andrew L. Robinson

Beattie McCleland

William H. Mallory

John Ryman

John L. Ketcham

Cromwell W. Barbour

Samuel B. Gookins

James Collins, Jr.

John Pitcher

Christian C. Nave

Andrew L. Osborn

Joseph W. Chapman

Jacob B. Julian

George W. Julian

James M. Hanna

Daniel D. Pratt

Godlove S. Orth

George W. Lawson

Stephen D. Dodge

Horace P. Biddle

Ebenezer Dumont

John S. Reid

James H. Henry

Oliver R. Doughterty

James Lockhart

Hervey Brown

Conrad Baker

Cyrus L. Dunham

Addison M. Crane

George Van Santvoordt

J.T. Preston

James Wilson

George Keeney

William H. Findley

Albert G. Porter

David Reynolds

Reuben Farnsworth

Lewis F. Moffatt

Lorenzo D. Dougherty

Frank Emerson

Asahel W. Hubbard

John A. Wilstach

Godlove O. Behm

Joseph R. Troxell

Nathaniel T. Hauser

Ezra A. McMahon

*Trusten B. Kinder

*Andrew M. Carnahan

John T. Hughes

John M. Cowen

John L. King

William A. Bickle

Napoleon B. Taylor

David M.C. Lane

Jonathon S. Harvey

Willis A. Gorman

Miles C. Eggleston

James Bradley

William B. Greer

John Davis

Robert L. Walpole

James E. Blythe

Horatio C. Newcomb

William Wallace

Orville S. Hamilton

John A. Matson

Addison L. Roache

William H. Stewart

Joseph K. Edgerton

John D. Howland

James Harrison

William Hendricks

Alvin P. Hovey

Lemuel Q. DeBruler

Charles Dewey, Jr.

Alexander C. Downey

Thomas B. Holcomb

Seth Smith

*James D. Glass

Hiram W. Chase

William B. Beach

Benjamin F. Myers

John C. Spencer

William C. Wilson

Martin L. Bundy

Thomas F. Thompson

William M. McCarty

James M. Reynolds

Davis Newell

William Henderson

William S. Holman

John Coburn

William M. Dunn

Theodore Gazlay

J.S. Scobey

Abram Brower

William A. McKenzie

George V. Howk

James P. Luse

Edwin Coburn

Thomas D. Walpole

Joseph Robinson

Reuben A. Riley

Clerk: H.P. Coburn   Sheriff: James H. Johnson

Photo courtesy of Indiana Supreme Court

"He was about five feet nine inches high, very erect, with a neat, trim, lithe figure; he was quick and active in motion and graceful in bearing."

Chapter III
The Man and the Judge

In other chapters yet to come we will discuss the opinions or judicial writings of Blackford, of him as a reporter and his reports, and his judicial associates, and this necessarily will somewhat limit this chapter.

There is one incident in Blackford's life not altogether satisfactorily accounted for.

Colonel George McDonald, when Blackford was a student in his office in Middlebrook N.J., had a daughter, Caroline, then a little girl, who often "had climbed upon his knees." She was a beautiful child. In 1819 Blackford revisited Somerville and renewed his acquaintance with Caroline, and the Colonel's family.

By some persuasion, it is not known what, McDonald was induced to give up his lucrative practice in Somerville and come to Indiana in the fall of 1819. He settled in Vincennes. In the spring of 1820, Blackford married Caroline, who was then only in her twentieth year, while he was fourteen years older. A year after her marriage (May 30, 1821), she died in childbirth. The marriage was an unfortunate one, for evidently she liked society but he did not. This conclusion may be drawn from the fact that he wrote his mother an account of the death and said he "would never marry again," and he kept his word. Caroline was buried at Vincennes.

The child was a boy. He died about 1835, though the date is uncertain. His death was a great blow to his father. His name was George, named after his grandfather Colonel George McDonald. He was buried at Lexington, Kentucky. Mr. Woolen says of this boy and his father's grief over his death:

> The father was wrapped up in his boy. He was not only an only child, but he was the only hope of perpetuating the Blackford name. This child and companion of the cloistered jurist, sickened and died while at Lexington, Kentucky, under medical treatment of Dr. Dundley. The father went to Lexington, and after seeing his boy laid away in his tomb, returned to his home. It was in the summer time and he reached Indianapolis in the middle of the night. Instead of going to his room in the Circle, he went to the residence of Henry P. Coburn, and, without knocking, opened the door and entered the house, a house in which he was ever welcome. Soon after, one of Mr. Coburn's sons was awakened by the stifled sobs of the mourner. He arose from his bed, and, lighting a candle, beheld Judge Blackford,

walking the floor and sobbing as though his heart would break. Not a word was said. The young man knew the cause of the great grief of his father's friend, and, having no wish to intrude upon its sanctity, left the room. Judge Blackford remained at Mr. Coburn's for several days, and during the time, held no conversation with anyone. He took his meals in silence and when they were over, returned to his room. When narrating this incident, General John Coburn said to the author: 'I have seen grief in all its forms; have seen the mother's mourning for her son; have seen the wife at the grave of her husband, and heard her sobs, but I never saw such appalling agony as Judge Blackford exhibited that night at my father's home.'[21]

Blackford had a room, after his son died, in the Governor's Mansion, located in the Circle, now known as "Monument Place." It stood where the Soldiers and Sailors Monument now stands. His room was plainly furnished, yet it contained everything necessary for comfort. There were three tables in it, and these were always loaded with books. A colored man (William Franklin, living in 1883) swept the room, made the fires, and did other necessary things about the house. He was Blackford's servant twelve years, and said that during that time he never saw him in a passion, nor heard him utter an angry word. He nursed him when he was sick, and attended to his little wants when he was well. He had the best opportunity to know him as he really was. In his room he lived almost like a hermit for twenty years.[22]

On one of his trips to Vincennes, Blackford came very near losing his life.

Mounted on a stout horse, with overcoat, leggings, and saddlebags full of law books, he undertook to ford White River, near Martinsville, while the river was much swollen by a freshet. He and his horse were swept down the stream a great distance, but eventually landed on an island. The judge was wet and cold, and it was several hours before he reached the main

---

[21] William W. Woolen, *Biographical and Historical Sketches of Early Indiana* (Indianapolis: Hammond & Co., 1883) 349.

[22] EDITOR'S NOTE: Thornton recounts these details from Woolen's biographical sketch of Blackford published in 1883.

land, being rescued by a farmer who heard his outcries. He spent a couple of days in drying his law books and clothing, and waiting for the water to fall enough for him to cross the river in safety, and then proceeded on his journey.[23]

Of his personal appearance, Woolen says; "He was about five feet nine inches high, very erect, with a neat, trim, lithe figure; he was quick and active in motion and graceful in bearing. His face was long, though well proportioned, and marked with intelligence, sensibility and refinement. His head was small but shapely."[24]

Blackford lived the greater part of his life alone, having the habits of a student and the tastes of a scholar. He was upright and scrupulously honest in his dealings, and was a model of integrity and character. He was a believer in the Christian religion, a regular attendant at the Second Presbyterian Church when Henry Ward Beecher was its minister, of whose oratory he was very fond. He was not a member of any church.

He had a mistrust of banks. His Vevay experience was responsible for this. More than once he let his salary as judge lie in the State treasury for several years. If the State paid in scrip, it drew six per cent interest. To some extent it may be said he was miserly in his habits. He seldom parted with any money without an equivalent, and was careful in its expenditure. He was not a benevolent man, and usually when he gave, it was to escape importunity, more than from a love of giving.

Woolen tells this story of him as an illustration of his habits in monetary matters:

> In March 1851, when Jenny Lind sang in the Madison Pork House, he went to Madison to hear her. There was much excitement the evening she sang over the sale of tickets, but he stood at the box office and patiently bided his time. When the bidding became slack, and when the price of tickets dropped to four dollars he made his purchase.[25]

---

[23] Woolen, *Biographical and Historical Sketches of Indiana*, 351.
[24] Woolen, *Biographical and Historical Sketches of Indiana*, 351.
[25] Woolen, *Biographical and Historical Sketches of Indiana*, 346.

For the times he had a large and miscellaneous library consisting of two thousand volumes or so. But they were chiefly legal works, for he took no interest in subjects not of a legal trend. Outside of the law he was not a learned man; though in early life he had a love for poetry (and perhaps the classics, for in these he had excelled in college), but that soon deserted him.

He was remarkably industrious and painstaking, working incessantly, having no set time in which to perform his judicial labor. In fact he was a drudge. Precedent with him was everything. He was decidedly a plodder, creeping at a snail's pace through whatever he had to do. He wrote and rewrote until he was satisfied with his opinion. When overcome with fatigue and nature's demand for sleep and rest, his head often fell forward on his desk, and after long and unremitting labor he would frequently sleep thirty-six or forty-eight hours without intermission.

The floor of his room was uncarpeted; and, it has been said, for years his bed lay on the floor. He took his meals at a cheap hotel; and lived for days on crackers and cheese, a supply of which he always kept by him. Shortly after the confirmation of one of his appointments, he gave a banquet to five of his Whig friends who had voted for him. The banquet consisted of two pounds of hard shell almonds, a few crackers, and a single bottle of champagne. He cracked the nuts on the floor with his heel.

Blackford owed, and owes yet, much of his reputation to his *Reports*, at least beyond the State lines. The first, second and third *Indiana Reports*, edited by other reporters, excellent scholars, do not add to his fame. With their publication he had nothing to do. As early as 1822, his attention was drawn to the advantages of a systematic report of the opinions of the Court, but he did not publish his first volume, extending over the first ten years of the Court, until 1830. One thousand copies were printed of the first volume; seven hundred and fifty (1834) of the second; one thousand each of the third (1836), fourth (1840), and fifth (1844); one thousand five hundred

"Blackford owed, and owes yet, much of his reputation to his Reports, at least beyond the State lines."

each of the sixth (1845) and seventh (1847); and one thousand two hundred and fifty of the eighth (1850).

All the opinions received his personal attention. That he revised the opinions even of his associates, is unquestionably true, but he was probably more lenient with those of his associates than his own. He studied the art of punctuation; and is said to have read the best books for style. A misplaced comma, in his opinion, was as inexcusable as a grammatical error. On one occasion an entire signature (sixteen pages) was printed four times before the punctuation suited him. When the eighth volume was going through the press he held up an entire printing house three days so that he could determine the correct spelling of the word "jenny," a female ass, not satisfied whether it should be spelled with a "g" or a "j." For this delay he paid one hundred and twenty-five dollars. During 1843, he paid his printer six hundred dollars for similar delays; and in the publication of the eighth volume, covering a period of over eighteen months, over eleven hundred dollars. He kept his proof sheets lying on a table in the Supreme Court library, with a request that all errors found be noted on blank paper kept with them for that purpose. On one occasion Albert G. Porter (who became Governor of the State in 1881) called his attention to the printed word "optionary," saying there was no such word. Several years afterwards he was appointed, very unexpectedly to himself, Reporter of the Supreme Court. Upon asking the Governor, who appointed him, why he did so, that official told him it was because Judge Blackford had urged his appointment, and solely because of the error he had discovered.

Samuel Judah was a lawyer located in Vincennes, and one of the leading lawyers of the State. The summer vacation of the Supreme Court was a day or two at hand, and he had a case in that court in which he desired its decision delayed until fall. There was a word he knew would have to be in the opinion, and he asked Blackford how the word should be spelled, not revealing however that the word would necessarily appear in the opinion. The Judge answered, giving the usual orthography; but Judah took issue with him and argued that the spelling was not correct. Blackford at once began a most careful examination of the word, dug out its roots and carefully weighed all the authorities he could find. He spent two days at this work, and before he got through, the Court adjourned, and the case went over to the Fall Term.

"Samuel Judah was a lawyer located in Vincennes, and one of the leading lawyers of the State."

So far as known Blackford's pen was only employed on his opinions, his reports and excellent notes he often inserted in his reports of his opinions. There is known a single exception. It is an address he delivered as presiding officer, before the American Colonization Society, December 31, 1829, on the subject of the negro, his condition in this country as a slave, and his condition in Africa, and his colonization in Liberia.

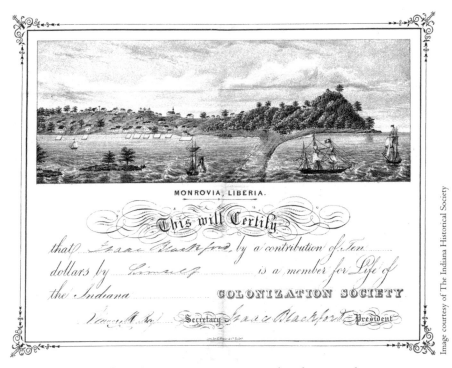

Blackford's Colonization Society Membership Certificate

Blackford was vice president of the National Colonization Society and president of the Indiana branch. At the first meeting of this branch, December 31, 1829, he delivered a long address, occupying an entire page of the *Indiana State Gazette.*[26]

The address is full of information concerning the negroes in this country, of the extent of slavery, of the colonization in Liberia and the progress there made in negro government. It is composed in fine style, a model of

> *"The address is full of information concerning the negroes in this country, of the extent of slavery, of the colonization in Liberia and the progress there made in negro government."*

---

[26] *The Gazette* was a weekly paper of only four pages, the pages being somewhat smaller than the ordinary newspaper of the present day.

writing. In the only editorial in the paper the editor says of it, "the style is chaste and elegant, the historical part of the unassuming writer."[27]

In 1825, without his authority, and without consultation with him, Blackford was nominated for Governor. His opponent was James Brown Ray, a good popular campaigner. Blackford was a very poor one, incapable of making a public political speech. And yet, in spite of his handicap, he received 10,418 votes to Ray's 13,040.

At the next session of the General Assembly, he was thrust forward as a candidate for the United States Senate. His opponent was Governor William Hendricks, who had been elected Governor in 1822, receiving all of the votes that were then cast, a most astute politician only rivaled by Jonathan Jennings. Blackford was defeated by only one vote, a striking testimony to his popularity. Of course he was then a Whig, and Hendricks a Democrat.

"At the next session of the General Assembly, he was thrust forward as a candidate for the United States Senator. His opponent was Governor William Hendricks, who had been elected Governor in 1822..."

Blackford in the early life was a Whig; and as such he came to Indiana. In 1824, he was an elector on the Adams ticket; in 1832 he voted for Clay, but in 1836 he supported Van Buren for the Presidency; and after that acted with the Democrats. He supported Van Buren against General Harrison. Slavery had been "covertly introduced" into the territory, and laws were enacted in aid of the practice. Congress had been petitioned to suspend the Sixth Article of the Ordinance of 1787 prohibiting slavery in the territory. Governor Harrison approved, not only of the "covert" laws, but also of the petition to Congress. Harrison had been a Virginian and Blackford a New Jerseyman. Yet Harrison

---

[27] *Indiana State Gazette*, 31 December 1829.

was a Whig, and notwithstanding that was a man in favor of slavery within the territory.

These "covert" laws, as they have been termed, authorized the bringing of negroes into the territory, and provided for apprenticing males until they were thirty-four years of age, and females until they were thirty-two years old. This law also provided that slaves found ten miles from home, without permission of their masters, might be taken up and whipped with twenty-five lashes. The law provided that children of colored people, born in the Territory, might be apprenticed until the males were thirty and the females twenty-eight years of age.

Of all these, as Governor of the Territory, Harrison approved. He was very much under the influence of the coquetry of the Virginia cliques who surrounded him.

But Blackford hated slavery; and, Whig though he was, he refused to support the Whig candidate Harrison for the presidency, and supported and voted for Van Buren, the Democratic candidate.

Blackford was reappointed judge of the Supreme Court in 1823, 1830, 1836, 1843 and 1850.

In 1823 his fellow associates James Scott and Jesse L. Holman, were also reappointed; but in 1830 Governor Ray refused to reappoint either of them notwithstanding he reappointed Blackford. He appointed Stephen C. Stevens of Jefferson County and General John T. McKinney of Franklin. Ray's refusal to reappoint Scott and Holman rendered him quite unpopular.[28]

McKinney died in office in May 1837; and Jeremiah Sullivan of Jefferson County was appointed May 29, 1837 to succeed him. Charles Dewey was appointed May 30, 1836, by Governor Noble.

Blackford, Dewey and Sullivan raised the Old Supreme Court to the

---

[28] In the sketches of Scott, Holmes, Stevens and McKinney, found in Chapter VI this is discussed more at length.

highest reputation it ever attained. They were its three greatest judges.[29]

Politics played its part in 1846. Blackford was a Democrat, and was reappointed as a matter of course. William L. Marcy a decade or so before had coined the sentence "to the victors belong the spoils." Governor Whitcomb refused to reappoint Dewey and Sullivan; and in their stead named Thomas L. Smith of Floyd County, a Democrat, to succeed Dewey, and Samuel E. Perkins, also a Democrat, of Wayne County, to succeed Sullivan. They continued in office until January 3, 1853, when the Old Supreme Court expired under the Constitution of 1851. In ability and reputation the Court declined [after it became popularly elected]; and its reputation would have been less than it was if it had not borne the reputation it attained under Blackford, Dewey and Sullivan.[30]

In later life Blackford lost his popularity and his popular hold upon the people, especially after his retirement from the bench in January 3, 1853. In 1852, he desired to be retained on the bench. This selection was then, under the new constitution, by popular vote. In the Democratic convention Samuel E. Perkins defeated him for the nomination, to the State's loss, and was elected, taking his seat, with the three other newly elected Judges, Andrew Davison[31] of Decatur County, William Z. Stuart of Cass County, and Addison C. Roache of Marion County.

Blackford even failed to get the nomination of Supreme Court Reporter. In 1852, Thomas A. Hendricks defeated him for the nomination for Congress.[32]

---

[29] See sketches of Dewey and Sullivan in Chapter VI.

[30] See sketch of Dewey in Chapter VI for an account of Governor Whitcomb's conduct in making the new appointments, and the Senate's in ratifying them.

[31] Not "Davidson" as some write his name.

[32] It took 32 ballots to decide the question. Afterwards becoming the Democratic nominee for State Senator he was defeated by the candidate of the People's Party. It seemed that his days of office holding were at an end. It has been said that he was a persistent office seeker. There is no doubt he coveted political honors but his political ambitions over reached his political ability. His successive political defeats left him completely disillusioned concerning his ability. Blackford took his defeat for Supreme Court judge bitterly, saying he would rather stay on the bench without pay than to leave it.

Blackford's reverence for judicial dicta at times led him astray. Thus in the State v. Tipton he wrote an opinion to the effect that the judgment of a court of competent jurisdiction respecting contempts could not be appealed from relying upon an English case.[33] For forty years this was the law of this State, until the question again came before the court when it was found that the English case was not at all on point, while the whole current of modern decision was the other way.[34]

In the case of Deming v. Bullitt[35] and in Cunningham v. Flinn[36] he held that a demand made before bringing an action for a deed, where the owners of the land had covenanted to convey as payment of the purchase money, and the money had been paid, in order to maintain the action, for a specific performance, was not necessary. A few years later, the question arose in Sheets v. Andrews[37] after Suyden's great work on "The Laws of Vendors and Purchases of Estates" had appeared; and on the strength of the statement of that eminent authority, Blackford overruled his two former opinions, holding that a demand first made was essential to maintaining the action.

So the case of Shanklin v. Cooper is another case of his reverence for precedent.[38] Twenty thousand dollars were involved. One person, Maynard French, had executed two notes in New York, made payable in a bank in that State, in favor of Shanklin, who, in Indiana indorsed them to Cooper. If the contract of indorsement was an Indiana contract, Shanklin was not liable under the facts developed at the trial; if it was a New York contract, he was liable. Judge Sullivan wrote an opinion holding that the contract of indorsement was an Indiana contract; but before he filed it in the clerk's office his term of office expired. The case was then assigned to Blackford

---

[33] 5 *Blackford* 166.
[34] In the Lord Mayor of London 3 *Wils* 188
[35] 1 *Blackford* 241.
[36] 1 *Blackford* 266.
[37] 2 *Blackford* 274.
[38] 8 *Blackford* 41. The decision swept away the fortune of the indorser.

who found that in <u>Rothschild v. Currie</u>[39] it had been decided that an indorsement was a contract which was governed by the law of the place where the note is payable, without regard to the place where the indorsement was actually made. This remained the law for fourteen years when the case in principle was overruled in <u>Hunt v. Standart.</u>[40]

Blackford's memory was also very deficient as demonstrated by the two cases of <u>Hawkins v. Johnson</u>[41] and <u>Vest v. Weir</u>[42], in which there is a direct conflict, notwithstanding a little over one hundred pages of the *Report* intervene between them, in which he prepared both opinions.

---

[39] 1 *Adolphus and Ellis*, New Series, 43.

[40] 15 *Ind.* 33. Blackford had refused to follow Story's *Conflict of Laws, Bills of Exchange*, and other American authorities. His love of and belief in the correctness of the English decision could not be shaken.

[41] 4 *Blackford* 21.

[42] 4 *Blackford* 135.

"Blackford's opinions are models of judicial writing.
They were written in the days of the quill."

Chapter IV
Blackford's Opinions

lackford's opinions are models of judicial writing. They were written in the days of the quill. They were not dictated to a stenographer, with whom it would seem many of the judges are having a merry race. Very, very few judges can condense when dictating an opinion to a stenographer; and once it is typewritten it is almost impossible for the judge's mind to review and condense it. The act of writing with a pen tends to condensation, to accurate expression, to clearness of statement better than any other method yet devised to secure desirable judicial opinions and judicial writing. But judges weary of the act of writing especially in the last fifty years. It is so much easier to call in a stenographer and run off a lot of sentences — sentences not infrequently not necessary to a decision of the case. In this way dicta creep into our judicial opinions—dicta that usually, or at least often, confront our judges, even the judge who wrote the opinion, much to his embarrassment.

Take the loquacious judge — the jury lawyer, if you please, who prides himself upon his ability to sway a jury who has come to the bench, it is most frightful to contemplate what he and a ready going stenographer — or even without a stenographer — when preparing an opinion, may write.

Blackford had none of the qualities of such a lawyer. He did not have to contend with such an undesirable habit.

Nor do you find him paraphrasing of an opinion — especially a former opinion in the same court — as so often is the habit of judges in modern times. Quotations are rare in his opinions.

He did not write to make a show; nor to lengthen his opinions. On the contrary there were evident efforts to condense and to shorten the opinion. He wrote and rewrote his opinions, until he was satisfied with them. But he did not have the literary grace of Sullivan, nor the forcible expression of Dewey. Yet his opinions are smooth in diction, without obscurity, contain no uncertain expressions; and are models of judicial writing.

Men of literature do not look admiringly upon the literature of the law. They point out that treatises on the law and judicial opinions are not elegantly written; and the language used is without grace. Naturally this must be so. Fine writing has no place in the law. The subjects discussed do not admit of it. Lawyers look with distrust whenever there is an apparent effort to do "fine writing." Fine writing is not often attempted. Coke had a style that is execrable; and yet he is the most renowned of law writers. Blackstone was a great improvement upon Coke in style and in diction; and yet the early English lawyers said he was inaccurate. The King James Bible is, as a translation, the most elegant translation ever printed. Yet scholars are pointing out that it is full of inaccuracies in the rendition of the original Hebrew and Greek. Elegance and smooth flowing periods seldom admit of exact expression. And it is exact expression the law demands.

Blackford says in his preface to his first volume of the *Reports* he has revised many of the opinions he was printing. How much he revised them is impossible to tell now. Perhaps he revised the opinions of his associates far less than his own; for judges are very jealous of revisions of their opinions. Much revision of their opinions would have got Blackford in disfavor with them.

There is a decided defect in the method we pursue in the selection of judges for our Supreme Bench. We never for an instance ask the question, Can the candidate accurately express himself? In other words, Can he write? Can he write a grammatical opinion? We assume that every man who is a lawyer can write an opinion worthy of our consideration. We do not ask the question, Can he draw distinctions? A judge on the Supreme Court once said to me of a fellow judge, "When," naming the judge, "takes out his ax something falls." An examination of the written opinions on file in the Clerk's office of our Supreme Court shows that one judge would write a whole page without capitalization except at the beginning of the page. Often the pages were not divided into sentences. Punctuation was often disregarded. But for the care of the Reporter the reputation of that judge would have been away below par. Another judge, that came heralded as a great lawyer, would, as it were, take a club and beat out the brains of the party against whom he decided the case.

It is all a false idea that any lawyer who has attained some standing as a lawyer can write an opinion of any literary merit worthy of serious consideration. But happily Blackford was not that kind of a lawyer. Blackford's opinions run through the first, second and third *Indiana Reports*, but his opinions therein reported have never attracted the attention that those in his own reports have. He did not report them and consequently did not rewrite them.

His opinions are short, usually more so than his associates. Often half or three quarters of a page is sufficient in length to dispose of a case. Two pages is about the average length of an opinion, leaving out the title and syllabi. He seldom wrote a long opinion. His longest opinion is an equity case – a subject in which he did not seem at home. It covers twenty-two pages.

Blackford was his own editor. The fame his opinions brought him is much due to that fact. If they had been reported by an "official" reporter they probably would have fallen into the slough of forgetfulness into which his opinions in the three *Indiana Reports* have fallen.

As Judge Howard points out:

> The decisions of our Supreme Court under the Constitution of 1816, as reported by Blackford, laid the foundation of the law of Indiana. The judges were little fettered by precedent. They are chiefly guided by British authorities; and this at once gave to *Blackford's Reports* a reputation for learning and originality. The opinions, as they come to us, are vigorous and simple expositions of the laws, in which principles and authorities are happily blended. They gave to Indiana jurisprudence large credit, not only in America but also in Europe; and Blackford was honored by the most learned in the law as a backwoods Coke or Littleton. Under the Constitution of 1851, the reports of Blackford have undoubtedly become somewhat obsolete and are no longer cited so often as formerly; but they must always remain a storehouse of legal learning, the foundation of Indiana jurisprudence, and a monument to the memory of Isaac Blackford and the other jurists whose opinions are there recorded and preserved...*Blackford's Reports*, consisting of eight volumes, comprise a selection of opinions in all the important cases decided by the Supreme Court of Indiana during the thirty-four years while he was himself upon the bench. He, therefore evidently, receives credit not only for his own decisions and opinions of many eminent jurists who sat on the bench with him.[43]

---

[43] Timothy Howard, "The Indiana Supreme Court with Some Accounts of the Courts Preceding It," *Northern Indiana Historical Society Publication* 3 (March 1900): 12.

Blackford relied very much on English decisions and English text writers. Thus in the seventh *Blackford* he cited the following English and two American text books.

Chilty Criminal Law	Chilty on Precedents
Archbold Civil Pleading	Coke's Reports
Coke on Littleton	Preston on Estates
Suyden on Vendors	Chilty on Bills
Blackstone's Commentaries	Bayley on Bills
Chilty on Pleading	Chilty on Contracts
Tidd's Practice	Comyn on Contracts
Williams on Executors	Mitford's Chancery
Phillips on Evidence	Story's Equity
Chilty's General Practice	Kent's Commentaries
Starkie on Evidence	Chilty on Descents

Blackford's opinions meet with favor in other state Supreme and Federal Courts. His opinions as reported in his own eight *Reports*, up to 1919, have been cited 3,417 times; and those in the first three *Indiana Reports* 782, making a total of 4,199 times they have been cited in other state Supreme and Federal reports. They have been frequently cited by the United States Supreme Court.

In states where the common law practice prevails at the present day they are frequently cited, as in Illinois; and his *Reports* are still in demand.

His opinions attracted the attention of the English courts, an unusual thing; for those courts, even today, very seldom cite American decisions, regarding their own decisions as all sufficient unto themselves.[44] Washington Irving, when Secretary of the American Legation at the Court of St. James, wrote home of Blackford's first volume of his *Reports*, "I meet with it frequently, and I am often asked as to the antecedents of its author, whose name is quite familiar at Westminster."

---

[44] "The principal characteristic of his mind," said an eminent lawyer, "is caution. He never guesses. He is emphatically a book judge. Declarations with him are nothing; precedent and good authority, everything."

Chapter V
Later Years – The End

For over thirty years, Blackford had been continuously on the bench, holding office, a servant of the people, with an annual salary steadily fixed; and nothing of a financial character to worry him.

He was now sixty-eight years of age – an age when most men think it is time to retire from serious business. He was then without clients; and probably with only a few commercial and business associates. He had reached an age when the commercial world thinks it is about time to put a lawyer on the shelf; for younger men in the law are more apt to be sought.

Moreover he experienced that phase of legal life that almost all lawyers experience on retirement from a judicial career: their clients are gone; some one else has them, and they will not return. The bar has absorbed the legal business; and usually if he gets any, he must get some other lawyer's clients.

The excitement of the courtroom is gone; the walls of his office are so close that it seems oppressive. Where every day on the bench he was accustomed to look upon a lot of faces, sometimes many who are there as witnesses or onlookers. That deference shown him while judge is very apt to slacken or even disappear.

The partisanship which a lawyer assumes in examining his client's case and presenting it to the court and jury usually deserts him, or is very much lessened.

Then nine times out of ten, he almost invariably finds himself not as apt, not so vigorous as in the days of his practice before assuming a judicial career. He usually is not as versatile as he then was; and not infrequently finds he is awkward in the trial of a case. His argument to the jury is usually apt to be less forcible than it was in his legal professional days.

All this is especially true if he has been long upon the appellate bench, where the case is committed to paper, where there are no adversaries – no give and take in oral argument – and what he has to say must be committed to paper. While the writing of opinions makes him more accurate in his expressions it has not the flexibility of language and ready speech that open oral discussion gives a lawyer.

For over thirty-five years Blackford had been writing opinions that were, not only written once, but frequently a number of times. They were gone over and over, changed and revised. They had passed through the censorship of editing them when committed to print and given to the world. Such a situation is discouraging to any lawyer who experiences it.

General Terrell narrates this amusing incident in Blackford's career after he left the bench and engaged in the practice. It must have been very humiliating to Blackford.

"One of his first cases," says Terrell:

> Was tried before a jury in the Marion Court of Common Pleas. Judge David Wallace was presiding. The testimony of both sides had been submitted, and as the day was far spent, court adjourned until next morning, when the attorneys were to make their arguments. Judge Blackford was on hand bright and early, apparently eager to proceed with the case. It was the first time in thirty-five years that he had appeared as an advocate before a jury. When the time came for him to make his argument he arose with some trepidation, and thrusting his hand into his coat pocket for the manuscript of his speech, discovered to his astonishment, that he had left it in his office. Without the document he was entirely helpless, and he was compelled to beg the indulgence of the court and jury until he could go out and get it, which he did as quickly as possible; but he was evidently much embarrassed and humiliated by the unfortunate circumstance. He read his remarks in a stumbling, monotonous way that probably made little impression on the minds of the 'twelve good and lawful' jurors, inasmuch as they brought in a verdict against him. It is not unlikely, that the mishap and adverse verdict had some influence in his retirement from practice in the courts.

Blackford opened his office in Indianapolis, on his retirement from the bench, for the practice of the law. In what place is not known. The room he had occupied in the "Governor's Mansion" in the Circle had to be given up. He had occupied it at least twenty years. It was his only home. The leaving of this "home" no doubt was depressing, for he was without a practice and without a family.

He did not long continue his efforts (if he made any is doubtful) to secure a practice, but soon retired. He longed to be again upon the bench; and his friends were anxious to see him there. He was not at home at the bar.

In less than two years time an opportunity to again ascend the bench came to him. On February 24, 1855, Congress created the Court of Claims, to sit at Washington, and pass upon monetary claims against the Government. Such claims had been a very trying thing for Congress to handle by means of its committees. Rank injustice was often done claimants; and gross frauds perpetrated upon the Government.

Blackford's friends immediately saw an opportunity for him to again assume a judicial role. His honesty, ability and uprightness of character were known to all. Neither Whig, Republican nor Democrat questioned them. His *Reports* had made him known to the legal profession throughout the United States. President Pierce, before he was elected President, was a lawyer of fine ability and extensive practice. In fact, his ability as a lawyer decidedly excelled his ability as a politician or statesman.

When the question of putting Blackford (a Democrat) upon the bench of the Court of Claims he readily assented; presented his name to the Senate, which without

"When the question of putting Blackford (a Democrat) upon the bench of the Court of Claims he readily assented; presented his name to the Senate, which, without question confirmed his nomination."

question, confirmed his nomination. President Franklin Pierce said there was no man better fitted to assist in the organization of the court than Blackford. He was appointed on the 3rd of March, 1855.

Blackford's associates upon the Court of Claims bench were John J. Gilchrist, formerly Chief Justice of New Hampshire; George P. Scarborough of Virginia, and Edward G. Loring of Massachusetts. Judge Gilchrist was presiding judge or Chief Justice of the Court. He died in April 1856, and after his death Blackford became the Chief Justice.

Few now recollect Blackford as a judge of the Court of Claims. His opinions given there have not attracted attention. This is only a necessary result of the peculiar character of the court.

Originally the court was created in the character of an advisory committee to Congress, with powers only to investigate claims and report the facts. Such reports did not call for a discussion of legal propositions.

The Daily Journal.

B. R. SULGROVE .... } Editors.
R. VAILE .... }

INDIANAPOLIS, THURSDAY, MAR 8, 1855.

Juage Blackford and the Court of Caims.

Messrs. Gilchrist of New Hampshire, Lumpkin of Georgia, and Blackford of Indiana, have been appointed Judges of the Court of Claims. These are said to be good apppoitments. Judge Montgomery Blair of Missouri, a son of Francis P. Blair, is appointed Solicitor. His nomination was strenuously resisted on account of his freesoil affinities.—*N. Y. Tribune, 5th.*

A later report says all of these appooitments were confirmed by the Senate. The Court of Claims will be the most important judicial tribunal in the country, except the Supreme Court of the United States. If we understand its duties correctly, it is to decide on all cases of claims against the government. They are cases generally involving immense sums of money, and often hampered with doubts and difficulties of a life time of neglect and delay. The duties will be very onerous, anfi the $4,000 per annum salary will be well earned.

Much of the time of Congress has been frittered away in considering these claims, and the establishment of the Court will save an immense expenditure of time and research and labor by our Representatives. It will more than likely be thrown away on other matters less important, it is true, but the Court will deprive them of at least one excuse for wasted time or hasty legislation. Furthermore, the transfer of these claims to a Court, where they will be heard and determined like other law suits, will destroy much of the bribery that has been so shamefully practised amongst our Representatives, by diminishing the need of it.

In a Court bad claims cannot be bribed through, any more than a murderer can bribe himself clear,—a very rare occurrence,—and the certainty that their cases will sometime be heard and settled, will remove all inducement for honest claimants to quicken action as in the case of Committees or the House, by largesses opportunely given to influential members. Speculators who have bought bad claims for the chance of winning, will feel very little disposed to press them when they have to pass the ordeal of three cool, clear headed "old fogies," who have a mortal aversion to acting upon anything till they know all about it, and when every step must be substantiated by testimony, instead of being established in a half-fuddled Congressman's brain by the summary, but satisfactory process of a bottle of Heidesick and a terrapin supper. It will make a great difference. "Private claims" will have passed into oblivion along with *paine forte et dure* and other modes of legal torment, as soon as the Court of Claims gets fairly under way.

Announcement of Blackford's appointment to the Court of Claims. Indianapolis Daily Journal, *8 March 1855.*

Necessarily, Blackford's appointment called for residence at Washington. There he died on the last hour of 1859. On January 4, 1860, both the *Indianapolis Sentinel* and the *Indianapolis Journal* announced his death, with fine editorials in appreciation of him as a man, a judge and a jurist. The General Assembly was then in session, and Governor Willard sent a message to it announcing his death. Subsequently he announced to the Democratic Convention then in session, that the body of the dead jurist had arrived in Indianapolis and would lie in state in the Senate Chamber. The body arrived January 13th and lay in state in the Senate Chamber which was draped in mourning. It was in a metallic casket, and was in a good condition. Most of the citizens of the city, and many strangers viewed the remains.

"Necessarily, Blackford's appointment called for residence at Washington. There he died on the last hour of 1859."

At 2 p.m. the funeral procession was formed by James Blake, master of ceremonies, and proceeded to the First Presbyterian Church, where Rev. M. Cunningham preached a funeral sermon. The pallbearers were E.N. Huntington, Calvin Fletcher, John Law, N.B. Palmer, John B. Newman, Allen Hamilton, Andrew Davison, James Morrison, Henry S. Lane, Abel C. Pepper, James M. Ray and Newman Eddy, all distinguished men of the day.

The committee of arrangements was Governor Willard, Stoughton A. Fletcher, Judge Roache, James Blake and Simon Yandes.

The present judges and also former judges of the Supreme Court, and Justice Hughes, Blackford's successor on the bench of the Court of Claims, attended the funeral and were in the funeral procession. Many of the citizens of the city and others joined in the procession. No one within the State had ever received so great a tribute by attendance at his funeral as Blackford that 13th day of January 1860 received.

Blackford's remains were first placed in a vault in Greenwood Cemetery. Crown Hill Cemetery at that time had not been founded.

In 1866 his body was removed to Crown Hill Cemetery and interred in a lot closely west of where the soldiers of the War of the Rebellion are now buried. Upon a monument erected to his memory at his grave is this inscription:[45]

---

[45] This monument is of white marble, over ten feet high, with a base over three and a half feet square. The same inscription or legend is on both the east and west sides, but badly worn by the weather. These inscriptions were probably cut 62 years ago. Woolen in his *Biographical and Historical Sketches of Indiana* (p. 347) says, "The above historical inscription closes with the following words, The honors, thus conferred were the just rewards of an industry that never wearied of an integrity that was never questioned." A personal examination made by the present writer shows that no other inscription is on this monument The only way the present writer can account for the mention made by Woolen, is that it was on the old grave stone or monument erected in Greenwood cemetery, and that he either copied it from that stone or copied the copy of some one else who copied it from the old tombstone or monument. The monument in Crown Hill Cemetery has all the appearance that it was first erected in that cemetery and not in Greenwood Cemetery.

ISAAC BLACKFORD L.L.D.

Born in Summerset [sic] Co. New Jersey Nov. 6, 1786.

Died at Washington D.C. Dec. 31, 1859.

Graduated from Princeton College in 1806.

Settled in Indiana 1811.

Was appointed Territorial Judge 1814. In 1817,
was appointed Judge of the Supreme Court which
position he held continuously for thirty-five years.

The author of Blackford's Reports.

In 1855, was appointed Judge of the
U.S. Court of Claims which office he held
at the time of his death.

On the day of the funeral a bar meeting was held at
Indianapolis in observance of his death. Judge Morrison presided. John L.
Ketcham, chairman, presented the following resolutions which were adopted:

> Resolved, That while we receive in the profoundest sorrow
> the announcement of the decease of the late Hon. Isaac
> Blackford, we cherish for his memory the highest regard,
> acknowledging that he has contributed more than any other
> man in Indiana to the high character of her judicial reputation;
> that such judges are a blessing to any state, and deserve to be
> held in great respect by all the people.

> Resolved, That we recognize in his removal the hand of
> God, and also acknowledge his goodness to the State in
> sparing so long one who presided over her highest judicial
> tribunal with such marked ability and spotless integrity.

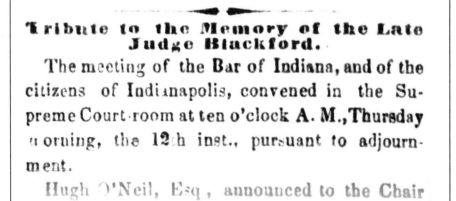

Report of bar meeting honoring Judge Blackford. <u>Indianapolis Sentinel</u>, *13 January 1860.*

On the death of Judge Blackford, a meeting was held at Washington of the Indiana Congressional Delegation. On that occasion Hon. Albert G. Porter (afterwards Governor of Indiana, 1881-1885), then of the Indianapolis district, in an address said:

> It is hardly possible, sir, for persons who reside in an old community to appreciate the extent to which, in a new country the character of a public man may be impressed upon the public mind. There is not a community in Indiana, not a single one, in which the name of Judge Blackford is not a household word. He was identified with our State from the beginning. He may almost be said to be a part of our institutions. Judicial ability, judicial purity, approaching nearly to the idea of the divine private worth singularly blending the simplicity of childhood with the sober gravity of age – these were present not simply in the mind of the profession, but in the universal popular mind of Indiana in the person of Isaac Blackford.
>
> Who has long known him can ever forget the magnitude and conscientious fidelity of his judicial labor; the modesty, which constantly disparaged those labors: the exalted purity of his private life, and the laugh which in the social circle in rare moments of relaxation seemed to ring more merrily than a child's?

While Judge Blackford held a place on the bench, no man, no chosen friend, no public body could ever elicit from him a private opinion upon any question of law. When he was written to by a suitor merely as to when a case would probably be decided, the letters were carefully folded in the transcript of the record, to be seen of all who might possibly be interested in the case.[46]

At the same meeting General William McKee Dunn said:

For more than a quarter of a century, Judge Blackford has occupied a seat on the Supreme Bench of our State. He has done more than any other man to build, our jurisprudence on the broad foundation of the common law. His Reports are not only an honor to him, but to the State of Indiana also. It has been well said here that he was an "upright judge" and not only was he so in fact, but so careful was he of his judicial character, and so regardful of all the proprieties of his position, that he was universally recognized and esteemed as 'an upright judge'.

Indiana is proud of her great jurist, but today she mourns the loss of one of her most eminent citizens, and now by her united delegation in Congress claims that all that is mortal of Isaac Blackford may be entrusted to her care and have sepulture in her bosom. Let his body be born back to the State with whose judicial history his name is inseparably connected, and thus at its Capital let him be buried, where those from all parts of the State who have so long known, revered and loved him may visit his tomb and pay affectionate tribute to his memory.[47]

We turn to what some of the newspapers had to say of Isaac Blackford in their obituaries of him. According to the *National Intellengencer*:

He made it a principle to owe no man pecuniarily or otherwise. Absorbed in his profession he mingled but little in society. He was reserved, and confided but little to any one. From this he was often wrongly judged and unjustly censured. In such cases a different judgment would have resulted, if the

---

[46] *National Intellengencer*, 6 January 1860.
[47] *National Intellengencer*, 6 January 1860.

reasons of his action had been known, but he seemed to prefer reproach rather than the publication of his troubles to the world. He was a pure man, pure from social vices, and simple in his life and tastes. He was unassuming, but exceedingly courteous in language and manner. To the young men in the profession especially, he was courteous and encouraging. He was a hard worker, patient in research and thorough in investigation.[48]

The *Indianapolis Sentinel* said:

He had thoroughly mastered the principles of common law. He was the pioneer in establishing the common law practice in Indiana not only, but throughout the West, and during his long career upon the bench he strictly adhered to it. Preeminently he was a common-law lawyer. He decided every case strictly upon established principles, by precedents and no one was more conversant with the decisions of the English common law judges. He held the scales of judgment evenly, uninfluenced by personal friendships or party affiliations. He was guided by the philosophy of the law, and he never left the beaten paths made luminous by the reported rules and principles of judicial decisions. He found the law, the established principle, and applied it to the case to be determined.[49]

And, the *Indianapolis Journal* said:

Preparing opinions and getting out reports were about the only features of a career of unusual evenness, and admirably suited the scholastic tastes and retired habits of the Judge. Buried in the little room in the upper story of the Governor's Mansion, he studied, wrote and read, and thus passed all that lifetime of a whole generation. Of course such a man was ill fitted to contend with the keen, energetic politician who had grown up since he became a recluse, and when the selection of Supreme Judges was passed over to the people he found himself nowhere in the struggle with his young associate Perkins.

Judge Blackford was not a man of great talents. His intellect though discriminating and logical, was not very

[48] *National Intellengencer*, 4 January 1860.
[49] *Indianapolis Sentinel*, 3 January 1860.

strong or acute. He spoke but little and that little very badly, hesitatingly, confused and not very coherent. He would have been over in an instant by any brasslunged spouter who should have ventured into debate with him. The last hours of his life were painfully diffident in any situation that exposed him to special attention. But in his room alone, with his facts in his transcript, and the law in his library, he was a giant, not in power but in production. Slowly, but with absolute certainty, he would dig on from point to point till he saw daylight through it. And when he went through a case there was never any need for another road till the present generation began guessing at the law, as Judge Wick expressed it. He was laborious, careful and above all conscientious. His legal opinions, as those of his great associates, Dewey and Sullivan are models of their kind, clear, compact and complete. They carried no weight of immaterial discussion, and they lost no weight through grammatical leaks or rhetorical cracks. Probably if his successors had aimed no higher they would have fallen no lower. The same qualities that made his opinions sound made his reports valuable. They are quoted in every State in the Union and even in England with as much respect as any reports ever produced in this country.[50]

Men differ concerning whether Blackford was a "great" man. In an article published in the *Southern Law Review* of 1880. The writer gives the idea that he was not a "great" man, but the facts given do not well sustain the assertion.[51] In intellect he is not the equal of Marshall, or even Dewey; nor in learning had he a breadth of knowledge possessed by Story or Kent. In diction and accuracy of expression none of these excel him. No cleaner cut nor accurate opinions can be found than his.

A recent author has thus compared him with other lawyers of his day at the bar of Indiana:

In comparison with a score of lawyers who practiced at

---

[50] *Indianapolis Journal*, 4 January 1860.
[51] D.S. Alexander, "Judge Isaac Blackford," *Southern Law Review* 6 (1880): 907-928.

his bar he would suffer, yet he, no doubt, made a better judge
than any of them would have done. In sheer mental strength
he was not equal to Dewey. In mental circumference he was
not equal to John B. Niles. In knowledge of the practice of
law he was far inferior to O.H. Smith. In profound
understanding of the civil law, Samuel Judah surpassed him.
In pure intellectual strength and vision which open up to a
lawyer the path over which society is traveling, George G.
Dunn surpassed him. In the law of commerce, Stevens
surpassed him. In trial procedure, it is probable Sample,
Eggleston, and McDonald were his superiors. And so we
might find others greater in a special field of the law, yet it
is perhaps just as true that in all these points combined he
excelled any one of them...He has been criticized as being
too cautious, too conservative. This is mere opinion, and may
be right. At least it cannot be answered, only denied. In his
court lawyers knew just about what the law was, and that is
certainly a healthy condition of the law. In face of the great
social changes, just beginning when he left the bench, it is
difficult to hazard what he would have done. His service to
the State was great and there is nothing to be gained by
attempting to discount it by saying he must have failed had
he served another third of a century.[52]

As has been stated elsewhere, the line of Blackford died. This no
doubt was a prime cause of his sorrow when his son died. All possibility
of perpetuating his name to posterity had ended – a general propelling
incentive to most men. No doubt the name of Blackford remains in New
Jersey near where Isaac was born and reared; for just across the river from
the present borough of Bound Brook, in Piscataway Township, many of
the Blackfords are buried in the Samptown Buryground near New Market.

Blackford left no money to charity. In this he was not singular, for in
the days of his decease gifts in America to charity were rare. The
Americans, as they have now, had not acquired the habit of giving to

---

[52] Monks, *Courts and Lawyers of Indiana*, 189.

charity. All his fortune went to his half-sister, Charlotte Teressa Coon, who married Daniel Dayton Condit. Charlotte died November 9, 1881.

At the time of his death, Blackford was estimated to be worth a quarter of a million dollars, a decided fortune in those days (1859); very few lawyers — especially judges — acquired such a fortune.

When he ascended the bench in 1817 his salary was only $750 but bearing in mind the purchasing power of a dollar in those days, and in a newly-opened up territory of the West, it was not so insignificant an amount. A dollar then in Indiana was probably the equal of four dollars in the present time (1930). Then at that day there was little temptation to spend money as compared with the times of the today. Blackford's needs were few; his habits were simple; after his son died, about 1833, he had no one to support but himself; and as we have seen, he lived in the simplest manner possible without being a miser. He said of himself once he did not know how to spend money. In 1837 his salary was $1,500, in 1852 $1,300. As we have seen, Blackford often let his salary lie in the State Treasurer's office; and if it was payable in State script, as was the practice in early days, it drew six percent interest, and thus the original was considerably increased.

Then his *Reports* brought him in considerable amounts. In the Constitutional Convention of 1850-1851 it was said that reporting the court's opinions was worth $1,500 to $2,000 a year.[53] Although this statement was made in debate by a responsible attorney, it was perhaps a bit exaggerated.

It has been estimated that in his thirty-five years while on the bench he received from his salary and his *Reports* total not to exceed $50,000.

In those days unless it was in the last ten years of his life, land was

---

[53] *Report of the Debates and Proceedings of the Convention for the Revision of the Constitution of the State of Indiana* Vol. 2 (Indianapolis: A.H. Brown, 1850) 1662.

very cheap, and it was the practice to make investments in it. Lawyers often followed that practice. Not infrequently that was the only way a fee of some size could be collected. Many lawyers of the twenties, thirties, forties, and even the fifties became relatively very well off; for lands purchased at a low figure were not only a safe investment, but one that was bound to increase in value with the rise in value of real estate owing to the rapid increase in population.

Blackford at his death was the owner of valuable real estate in the city of Indianapolis, in at least three squares. He owned the lot at the southeast corner of Washington and Meridian Streets, on which now stands the Merchants National Bank (1930). On this lot he erected a four story building, known to the public as "Blackford's Block."

Chapter VI
Blackford's Judicial Associates

During the thirty-five years, Blackford was on the bench of the Old Supreme Court the following were his Judicial Associates:

James Scott.............................December 28, 1816 to December 28, 1830.

Jesse L. Holman.....................December 28, 1816 to December 28, 1830.

Isaac Blackford.......................September 10, 1817 to January 3, 1853.

Stephen C. Stevens ....January 28, 1831 to May 1836.

John T. McKinney.................January 28, 1831 to May 1837.

Charles Dewey.......................May 30, 1836 to January 1847.

Jeremiah Sullivan ....May 29, 1837 to January 21, 1846.

Thomas L. Smith..................January 29, 1847 to January 3, 1853.

Samuel E. Perkins ....January 21, 1846 to January 3, 1853.

January 3, 1853 to January 3, 1865.

January 3, 1877 to December 17, 1879

A short sketch of each of them may be of interest.

John Johnson[54]

John Johnson was not a judicial associate of Blackford on the bench. In a note preceding his opinions of his first report, Blackford says of him: "In the course of the preceding vacation, the honorable John Johnson, one of the judges of this court died at his residence in the County of Knox, universally esteemed as an honest man, and as an independent, intelligent judge."

Johnson was a native of Kentucky but it is not certain when or where he was born.[55] He was an advocate of slavery. As early as 1809 he settled at Vincennes and at once began the practice of law. Johnson took an active part in the election of that year, favoring the Indiana Territory passing to the second grade. In this he was associated with Benjamin Parke, Governor William Henry Harrison, John Rice Jones, Francis Vigo, Henry Hurst and General W. Johnson. In 1805, he was a member of the Territorial Legislature and as such joined in the petition to Congress to change the Ordinance of 1787 so that slavery might be brought into the Territory. He was selected with John Rice Jones, 1806 to revise and codify the Territorial Laws. This revision was adopted by the Legislature in 1807, and published in a thick, stubby volume, a book that is now very rare and commands a price of more than one hundred dollars. This revision now goes by the name of *John Rice Jones Revision*, but it is impossible now to tell which took the leading part in the work of completion. In 1809, when John Randolph, the pet of the Harrison faction, and a rabid slavery advocate, was pitted against Jonathan Jennings, the antislavery candidate as territorial delegate to Congress, Johnson was the third candidate. He received only eighty-one votes out of 911. The same year he was again candidate for the Territorial House of

---

[54] John Johnson has no known portrait.
[55] Dunn says he was a Virginian. Jacob Piatt Dunn, *A History of Indiana* (New York: Charles Scribner's Sons, 1916) 209.

Representatives. He was well known and popular, for he received more votes than any of the other five candidates, two of whom were to be elected. He received 203 votes. As Jennings had received 428 votes for delegate to Congress and Randolph 702, Johnson seems to have retired from politics. Johnson was a delegate to the Constitutional Convention of 1816, and "was probably the best lawyer in the Territory."[56]

He was the representative from Knox County at the Constitutional Convention. He was the head of the committee on distribution of the powers of government, and associated with him was Charles Polke of Perry County, Davis Floyd of Harrison County, David H. Maxwell of Jefferson County, and Enoch McCarty of Franklin County. As chairman of his committee he reported the clauses of the constitution relative to the division of power. The *Journal of the Convention* shows that he took a leading part throughout the twenty days it was in session.

In the congressional election of 1809 Jennings was the popular candidate of the eastern part of the State, and Randolph of the western part; so that Johnson being a Knox man, and a slavery man, like Randolph, drew votes from Randolph, thereby aiding and securing Jennings' election. Jennings did not forget the favor thus received; and when he became Governor of the new State, on December 28, 1816, appointed Johnson one of the judges of the Supreme Court just created. He died September 17, 1817, never having a chance to deliver an opinion, for no opinion was delivered by the Court for the term during which he served. He died before the maturity of his powers and the culmination of his usefulness. All his contemporaries speak highly of him as a man and of his legal ability.

---

[56] Dunn, *A History of Indiana*, 301.

Image courtesy of Indiana Supreme Court.

James Scott

As early as 1810 Scott was residing in Clark County; for in that year on December 14, he was appointed as a delegate to the Territorial House of Representatives, of which he became Speaker. On June 19, 1813, he was appointed Judge of the Chancery Court of the Territory, taking his seat April 6, 1813; and he then resigned his office as delegate to the Legislature.

He was a delegate from Clark County to the Constitutional Convention of 1816, with Jonathan Jennings, Thomas Carr and John H. Graham. He served on the committee relative to the judiciary department of government with John Johnson of Knox County, James Dill of Dearborn County, Samuel Milroy and William Lowe of Washington County, James Noble of

Franklin County, and William Cotton of Switzerland County.

Scott was appointed to the Old Supreme Court December 28, 1816 and served until December 28, 1830. He wrote ninety-seven opinions.

As we have seen, he was the victim of Governor Ray's temper, who refused to reappoint him and Holman, though he did reappoint Blackford.

Scott was a Pennsylvanian, "one of the purest men in the state" says Oliver H. Smith.

> A scholar and a fine lawyer. The opinions of no judge of our Supreme Court up to the present day (1857) are, I think, entitled to stand higher with the profession than his. A strong common-sense view of the case enabled him to select the grain of wheat from the stack of straw, and say, holding it up to the parties, without discussing the chaff, 'it is my opinion that this is a grain of wheat'.

Of Scott, General John Coburn said:

> A stout, rugged, and burly man, with a florid complexion, blue eyes, square face and a large head, indicating physical strength, a firm purpose and sound common sense. A plain spoken man, with a view of humor and pleasantry. In all respects for the bench, in a new country, where a strong sense of equity, and upright character and a good knowledge of the general principles of the law enabled him to attain to great eminence as a just and pure judge. He served fourteen years on the Supreme Bench, and retired with the unbounded confidence and respect of the Bar and people.

He was succeeded by Stephen C. Stevens in 1831.

"...a strong sense of equity, and upright character and a good knowledge of the general principles of the law enabled him to attain to great eminence as a just and pure judge."

Image courtesy of Indiana Supreme Court.

Jesse L. Holman

J esse L. Holman was born at Danville, Kentucky, that center of Territorial education and culture on October 2, 1787. When an infant his father was killed by the Indians. His widowed mother was able to give him a good commonschool education, sufficient to enable him to teach school or to preach. These professions were not attractive to him, so he turned to the legal profession, and read law in the office of Henry Clay. Before beginning the study of law he wrote a novel entitled "The Errors of Education." It was a two-volume work. Afterwards, becoming dissatisfied with it, he burned all the copies he could secure. He began to practice law at Carrollton, Ky.

He evidently inherited considerable property, becoming the owner of a number of slaves. Slavery was distasteful to him; for at the age of twenty-six he moved to Indiana, bringing his slaves with him, thereby freeing them. He settled on a farm near Aurora, Indiana, and there lived during the remainder of his life.

In 1814 he was elected as a representative to the Territorial Legislature. He resigned the office the same year in order to accept the appointment of Judge of the Second District of the Territory. December 26, 1816, he was appointed judge of the Old Supreme Court, serving two terms until December 28, 1830.

In 1831 he was a candidate before the State Legislature for the United States Senate, to succeed his old friend General James Noble who died that year in Washington. John Tipton defeated him by a single vote. Until 1835 he held no office. On the death of Benjamin Parke, the first judge of the United States District Court for Indiana, he was appointed judge of that Court, and held the office until his death, March 28, 1842.

Holman was one of several who laid out the town of Aurora, a rival of Lawrenceburg. He not only took a deep interest in schools of that town and the County of Dearborn, but also in the organization of Indiana University, being one of the trustees for twenty years.

Opinions differ as to his qualifications as judge. General John Coburn, who knew him, said, "he was a great judge, careful, laborious, and exact." Judge Timothy E. Howard, judge of the Indiana Supreme Court (1893-1899), says of him, and Judge Dewey, in his "Sketch of Supreme Courts," that they were undoubtly "The two greatest of the judges that sat with Blackford." Justice McLean, of the United States Supreme Court said, "his mind was sound and

"...his mind was sound and discriminating; of his legal record and acumen, he has left enduring evidence; but what most excited my admiration was his singleness of heart."

discriminating; of his legal record and acumen, he has left enduring evidence; but what most excited my admiration was his singleness of heart." Oliver H. Smith, a fair judge of men and lawyers, said, "A good lawyer, and one of the most just and conscientious men I ever knew."

Coburn said:

> Taking him all in all, he was a very remarkable man — a strong writer, a good speaker, pleasant and entertaining in conversation and observance of all of his duties as a neighbor and a citizen. He was a man of stout frame, a little inclined to stoop, with an ample head and drooping forward, as if in thought, with large, plain, regular and ample features, on which were stamped the kind and generous impulse of his nature. He passed through life without an enemy.

Yet in Monk's *Courts and Lawyers of Indiana* it is said, "as the judge of the State Supreme Court he can hardly be said to rank with the leading jurists." He wrote one hundred and thirty-eight opinions. He was a Baptist, serving as pastor of the Aurora Baptist Church during most of his life, without salary; and did more financially than any one else to support the church. His son, William S. Holman, served several terms in the United States House of Representatives and gained the sobriquet, "The Watch Dog of the Treasury."

Image courtesy of Indiana Supreme Court.

Stephen C. Stevens

Stevens was appointed judge of the Supreme Court January 28, 1831 and served until May 1836, when he resigned and Judge Charles Dewey was appointed in his place.

He came with his mother to Brookville before 1812. At the first session of the Territorial Court, held at Brookville, June 22, 1811, he was indicted for selling a tin pan to an Indian. This indictment was quashed. He made a business trip to New Orleans during the winter of 1813-1814, where he joined the Federal Army under General Jackson. At the battle of New Orleans, January 8, 1815, he received a musket ball in the head that troubled him all his life, and perhaps caused his insanity in his old age. His service in the army seems to have put him in better favor with the Franklin bar for, notwithstanding his having been indicted, he was admitted to that bar March 3, 1817.

He appeared in public life as a member of the Legislature from Franklin County, and was, strange to say, chairman of the committee for the revision of the laws.

At that time Brookville was pretty well occupied by lawyers, and he moved to Vevay. Stevens was a man of high temper. The court docket of 1817 shows that he and Senator Noble engaged in a fight in open court, and both drew fines of five dollars each.

In 1823 he was a member of the Legislature from Switzerland County; in 1824 again a member, he served as Speaker, and in 1826, he was elected to the State Senate, serving during 1828, 1829 and 1830.

At Vevay he drifted into business again, and organized the Vevay branch of the State Bank being its president and Isaac Blackford its cashier. The bank failed and he took up again the practice of law.

When he finished his term in the Legislature he was appointed judge of the Supreme Court. This seems due to two things — he was on friendly terms with Governor Ray and took his side of the controversy when he reorganized the Supreme Court.

Stevens enjoyed a wide practice, chiefly in collections. In 1836 he moved to Madison; and after his retirement from the bench he resumed the practice with success, somewhat in the nature of a modern collection agency. Madison was then the commercial city of the State; and Stevens prospered, accumulating a good fortune for that day. In 1852 this was swept away in an unsuccessful railroad promotion. The loss unbalanced his mind; and in 1869 he was placed

"Stevens was not a great Judge; in fact scarcely above mediocrity. A fine illustration of politics or favoritism putting a mediocre man on the bench."

in the State Hospital for the Insane at Indianapolis where he died a pauper, November 7, 1870.

Stevens was not a great judge; in fact scarcely above mediocrity. A fine illustration of politics or favoritism putting a mediocre man on the bench.

Nor was he a great lawyer, although he stood high with the bar. "Commercial lawyers" are seldom great lawyers. But his painstaking care and industry made him a successful practitioner, and he possessed considerable power before a jury. As a writer of pleadings and opinions he was diffuse and prolix, and his opinions contain many *obiter dicta.* Yet he was one of the most laborious judges that ever sat on the Supreme Court bench. He wrote seventy-one opinions

John T. McKinney[57]

"a fair lawyer, and gave good satisfaction as a judge, but died before he had reached the meridian of his life..."

Judge McKinney was another member of the reorganized Supreme Court. He was born at Brookville and there formed the acquaintance and friendship of Governor Ray. He was admitted to the bar March 15, 1815. Hendricks, Noble, McKinney, Stevens, Eggleston and Amos Lane did the bulk of the business at the Brookville bar. McKinney, according to his contemporaries, was the equal at the bar of any of these men.

He did not appear often in the Supreme Court, if we may rely upon *Blackford's Reports.* Little is known of McKinney's boyhood and early life. Yet he evidently was popular with the people, for he served two sessions as representative and three as senator, entering the legislature in 1826, and

---

[57] John T. McKinney has no known portrait.

serving consecutively until 1831 when he was appointed judge, making in all twelve years of public service. He died in office in May, 1837, and was succeeded by Sullivan.

Oliver H. Smith said of him in his *Early Indiana Trials*, that he was "a fair lawyer, and gave good satisfaction as a judge, but died before he had reached the meridian of his life or had been long enough on the bench to develop fully his judicial character. His opinions are sound law."[58] He wrote sixty-six opinions and was succeeded by Judge Sullivan.

---

[58] Smith, *Early Indiana Trails*, 145.

Image courtesy of Indiana Supreme Court.

Charles Dewey

W ith the appointment of Judge Dewey and Judge Sullivan, the Old Supreme Court regained the reputation it held before its reorganization by Governor Ray.

Charles Dewey was the strongest member, naturally and intellectually, of that Court, and at least the equal of any member of the New Supreme Court to the present day (1930). He was a New Englander of pronounced distinction. Born at Sheffield, Massachusetts, March 6, 1784, he was less than two years older than Judge Blackford. He was a well educated man, having graduated at Williams College with the honors of his class. After leaving college he studied law, and in 1816 came to Indiana and settled at Paoli, Orange County, where he opened an office and began the practice of law. He was remarkably successful, for he had a large business for that day, not only in his own county, but in adjoining counties. Those were the days when the lawyers rode the circuit and took cases whenever offered them.

On the records of the United States District Court for Indiana, at the second term held at Corydon, he was admitted to practice law there on November 3, 1817. He certainly soon was rated high as a lawyer for Governor Jennings retained him in 1818 as his Indiana counsel in his contest with Christopher Harrison over the possession of the Governor's office.

Dewey's first case in the Supreme Court, as reported in *Blackford's Reports,* came before the Court in 1818. It was over an eight hundred dollar note. The case was appealed from Clark County and was reversed. From thence on he appeared in that Court, until he assumed the bench. His practice covered that part of the State south of the National Road and west of a line running from Madison to Indianapolis. His principal competitors were Samuel Judah of Vincennes, Jude Hall of Princeton, Harbin Moore of Corydon, Calvin Fletcher of Indianapolis and Reuben S. Nelson of New Albany; and he was repeatedly opposed by James Whitcomb, the best prosecuting attorney on the circuit in the State.

Dewey was elected to the Legislature in 1821, from Orange County. The following year he was candidate for Congress against William Prince of Princeton. Prince had been a follower of Aaron Burr on his wild flight down the Ohio and Mississippi; and he defeated Dewey on the ground that Dewey had been a member of the Hartford Federalist Convention. As between the follower of Burr and a member of that convention, the honors were easy; but the pioneers of Indiana were more antagonistic to that convention than to Burr's filibustering expedition; and although Dewey had not been a member of the convention the charge was enough to defeat him.

In 1824 he removed to Charlestown, Clark County and there remained until his death. He served as United States District Attorney of Indiana from 1821 to 1829. He took no particular interest in politics yet he ran in 1832 for Congress against John Carr and was beaten. May 25, 1830, Governor Noble appointed him judge of the Supreme Court, to succeed Judge Stevens, who had resigned.

Dewey served as judge until 1847, when Governor Whitcomb was in office. In politics Dewey was a Whig and Whitcomb a Democrat. When the term of the three judges, Dewey and Sullivan (Whigs), and Blackford (Democrat), expired Whitcomb sent to the Senate the name of Blackford to succeed himself, and those of Samuel E. Perkins and Thomas L. Smith, both Democrats. The Senate confirmed the appointment of Blackford, but refused to confirm the appointment of either Perkins or Smith. Then followed a long and acrimonious contest between the Governor and the Senate over these appointments.

Whitcomb then sent to the Senate the names of several other lawyers, but they were all promptly rejected. After the Legislature adjourned, Whitcomb gave Dewey and Sullivan temporary appointments to last until the meeting of the next Legislature. When that body convened, the Senate promptly refused to confirm the Governor's nominees. A few days after it had adjourned, Whitcomb sent Dewey another temporary appointment. Before accepting it he had an interview with the Governor, and told him he would decline the appointment unless he had assurance that he would be regularly nominated and recommended to the next Senate. Whitcomb told him that he would, as a compromise measure, nominate him and Perkins to the next Senate, "unless he should be diverted from his purpose in respect to him [Dewey] by the course the Whigs might take in the coming canvass for Governor." It was undoubtedly his intention at that time to reappoint Dewey, but he was diverted from his purpose mainly through the influence of Ashbel P. Willard, just then rising to influence and power in the politics of Indiana. Dewey, being a Whig, was fiercely antagonized by the rising young Democratic politicians. Willard succeeded in preventing the nomination of Dewey, and in securing that of his friend and fellow townsman, Thomas L. Smith. At that time many thought this was done at the expense of Whitcomb's good faith.

In February 1847, Dewey in a letter to the *Indianapolis Journal* recounted at length his complaints against Whitcomb, giving the several interviews with him, and closed with the words, "I have only to add that the Governor's word has not been kept; his pledge is unredeemed."

On leaving the bench, Dewey resumed practice, taking with him as a partner, George V. Howk. They had a large practice throughout southern Indiana, as well as in the Supreme Court, Dewey's reputation bringing them business far and near. In April 1849, while riding in his carriage, he was thrown out and suffered a fracture of his leg. From this hurt he never recovered, being compelled during the remainder of his life to walk with crutches, but he continued to practice his profession while he lived.

Jonathan Jennings was his neighbor; and he was Jenning's legal advisor. Benjamin Parke, the first United States District Judge of the District of Indiana, and he were friends, and usually came to Indianapolis together, when business called them there, though they lived many miles apart. Dewey was a great reader of novels, but he could not persuade Parke to read them. After Parke's death, Dewey, at the request of the bar of the State, delivered an address upon his distinguished friend worthy of the distinguished subject. The clean cut sentences of his eulogy on Parke recall the writings of Burke. In it there is no superfluity of words; and the same may be said of Dewey's legal opinions. He, however, was not blessed with the graces of oratory. If he had been probably his opinions would not have been so good. Yet Dewey could talk with sense and fluency, and was very effective when presenting his views in court.

Dewey was fond of anecdotes. Having known personally nearly all the leading Indiana men of his day, he was full of reminiscences and stories, which he was in the habit of recounting to attentive listeners. But when on the bench, he was dignified and somewhat austere; but when off the bench, he was always ready to tell a story.

He was a member of the Presbyterian Church when he died. He was large and commanding, being six feet tall and weighing about two hundred pounds. His hair was black, in early manhood turning gray; his complexion dark; his forehead high and broad, and his mouth very expressive. Yet his features were not regular, his nose and chin being too long to be symmetrical, but his look of intelligence and dignity always pervaded his face and overcame these defects.

General John Coburn, who knew Dewey personally, says of him in *Indiana Bench and Bar*:

> He was a profound thinker, an able accurate reasoner, and able to grasp and master any subject submitted to him. He had strong friends and bitter enemies, for he was bold of speech and prompt in action, letting the consequences take care of themselves. He lived simply and plainly in a village and seemed never to covet either wealth or fame, and was entirely devoid of greedy ambition that disgraces and defaces so many other wise lofty characters. A more unselfish and unassuming man who could not be found, nor one with more utter scorn and contempt looked upon those who intrigued for office and honors at the hands of the people.
>
> To say that he was a great man intellectually is only to repeat what was awarded him by the common consent of all who knew him. Had he been elected to the United States Senate, or placed upon the Supreme Bench of the nation,

"He was a profound thinker, an able accurate reasoner, and able to grasp and master any subject submitted to him. He had strong friends and bitter enemies, for he was bold of speech and prompt in action..."

those who knew him felt that he could have stood worthily by the greatest and shared their labors and divided their honors. He was content to live in comparative obscurity, and to do the drudgery of a county court lawyer and wade through the hard and dry details of a judge of our early Supreme Court. He lived in a very great period of our history, while the nations were at peace, while violent popular agitation was discountenanced and before the vast upheavals of the rebellion had made opportunities and developed honors that gave enormous prominence to men greatly inferior to him. He lived in times when the fierce passions of the nation were lulled to repose after the two wars with Great Britain. It was the age of compromises, of financial disasters, of dull and tame progress. The agitators were told to hush. Jackson, Clay, Webster, and other powerful friends, in both parties, denounced the Abolitionists and the Nullifiers. Dewey was a Whig and one day in speaking of the Abolitionists, said, 'their tongues ought to be split'. He was not a reformer or an agitator. He waited for the clock to strike. He lived to hear it and stood by his country.

As a judge he had no superiors in America. He ranks with the highest. His style, his strong logic, his true sense of justice, and equity, appear in his opinions. He did not write them for display of his learning; he did not write essays on elementary law, when called on to simply decide one or two points; he refused to ramble over all the possible points of the case, in order to spin out an opinion. Of an old friend he once asked the question, 'Do you know why I do not write longer opinions?' On receiving an evasive answer, he said: 'I don't know enough to write long opinions; it is as much as I can do to write short ones on the few points arising in the case. If I can give one good reason for a decision why should I hunt for more? I think I can do well if I can do that much'. He could condense a thought or a sentiment as well as Horace, or a legal argument as well as Edward Deering Mansfield or John Marshall.[59]

---

[59] Taylor, *Indiana Bench and Bar*, 38.

When the Whig party dissolved he became a Republican. Two of his sons and two of his grandsons did valiant service for the Union cause during the Rebellion. Three of them died soon after the war from wounds and exposure. One son was a colonel from Iowa. His two grandsons were captains from that state. His other son was a lieutenant from Indiana.

Dewey died April 25, 1862, and was buried at Charlestown. He wrote three hundred and eighty-three opinions. His daughter, Eleanor, was married to George Vail Howk.

As a sample of Dewey's style, I make the following extract from one of his opinions.

According to Statute, "The President of the Circuit Court was empowered to hold court in another circuit for one term, or for a single trial, whose president was absent."[60] It was claimed this section was unconstitutional. Judge Dewey wrote the opinion holding it valid, and this opinion is a very fair staple of his judicial writing. "We are by no means," he said:

> Prepared to say that any part of the constitution, either in letter or spirit, so restrains the general authority of the legislature, as to prohibit it from passing the statute which we have under consideration if, indeed, the framers of the Constitution had rendered it necessary, that the Supreme Court should try capital cases when the president of a circuit in which they may happen is interested or prejudiced, they would have entailed upon the county a very serious evil. The necessity of bringing juries, and witnesses, and parties from the remote parts of the State to the seat of government, the expense, the delay, the trouble, the great uncertainty in the administration of justice, attendant upon such a trial, would produce a state of things which ought to be avoided if possible. The law in question does not avoid it. Besides this law has been in force for years. Many important decisions in

---

[60] *Indiana Revised Statutes* (1838), Chap. XXIII, Sec. 13.

chancery, and some in capital cases, have been made in Courts organized under it. If it be unconstitutional all such proceedings are void. The consequences are evident. Before we can consent to open a door to them, we must have the fullest conviction that stern duty demands it. We have not that conviction. We are not satisfied that the general authority of the legislature is so trammeled by any portion of the constitution, as to be incompetent to pass this beneficial law. We had this subject under consideration on a former occasion, and after much reflection came to the same conclusion which we now express. If the views here advanced do not leave the constitutional question in regard to this law free from all difficulty, we feel well assured they involve it in too much doubt to authorize us to declare the statute a nullity.[61]

---

[61] <u>Beauchamp v. State</u> 6 *Blackford* 299, 305. At the Cass County Bar memorial meeting, held at Logansport on the death of Judge William Z. Stuart one of the first judges under the Constitution of 1851, Judge Horace P. Biddle, then on the Supreme Court Bench, in his address, said that Stuart's opinions very closely resembled those of Dewey, of whom he spoke in the highest terms.

Image courtesy of Indiana Supreme Court.

Jeremiah Sullivan

On May 29, 1837, upon the death of Judge McKinney, Governor Noble appointed Jeremiah Sullivan his successor. Mr. Woolen prefaces his sketch of Judge Sullivan with these words: "Among the men who impressed themselves upon the morals of the people and institutions of the State in early days was Jeremiah Sullivan. He had much to do with laying the foundations of the State Government and in giving character to its judiciary, and he well deserves a place in the list of its distinguished men."

As his name indicates, he was of Irish descent. He was born at Harrisonburg, a small Virginia town, on July 21, 1794. He was educated at William and Mary College, from which he graduated with honors. His father urged him to become a priest in the Catholic Church on his graduation but he chose the profession of the law. Before being admitted to the law he joined the army and soon received a captain's commission. This was during the War of 1812. When the War was over he resumed his legal studies and soon after was admitted to the Virginia Bar; but his chances of rising there were meager and he determined to seek a more inviting field. So he started west on horseback for Louisville, Kentucky. When he arrived in Cincinnati he heard that Madison, Indiana was a good opening for a lawyer, so he changed his mind and went to that town. This was in the Fall of 1817 and there he settled and lived until he died. Even at that date, Madison had some of the leading men of the State; and with these he allied himself. In December 1817, he attended the meeting of the Masons at Corydon when the Grand Lodge was organized. Alexander Meek of Madison was elected Deputy Grand Warden and Sullivan Grand Orator. Subsequently during the Morgan era of disturbance he withdrew from the Masonic order and never rejoined it.[62]

In 1819 he was elected to the General Assembly and reelected in 1820. He proved himself to be an industrious and painstaking member, and was as influential in shaping legislation as any member in the House. It was he who proposed the name of Indianapolis for the capital city. In 1824 he made an unsuccessful race for Congress against William Hendricks, and this defeat seemed to have cured him of politics and caused him to adhere more closely to his profession. After this he never was a candidate for office at the hands of the people until the year in which he died.

Judge Sullivan, notwithstanding his Catholic origin, was a member of the Presbyterian Church. On the division of that church he allied himself with the New School branch. He was an active member of the church, becoming a ruling elder.

"He," says General Coburn, "was a careful, laborious and patient

---

[62] EDITOR'S NOTE: Thornton is referring to William Morgan (1774-?) who sought to publish Masonic rituals after being refused admittance by local lodges in New York. Morgan mysteriously disappeared while in jail in 1826. He was never seen again. A body was found in the area about a month later, but its identity has never been firmly established. Many believed that Morgan was murdered by Masons for his transgressions.

investigator of his cases and a constant student of the general principles of his profession."[63]

In 1829 he was appointed to represent Indiana in the attempt to devise a plan for building a canal from Wabash to Toledo. This required a working agreement between Indiana and Ohio for the adjustment of land claims growing out of the construction of the canal. He served as commissioner for several years in this adjustment.

It was as judge of the Supreme Court, from May 29, 1837 to January 21, 1846, that he gained his fame; and it is by that record he is now known by the profession. His opinions appear in the Fourth, Fifth, Sixth and Seventh *Blackford's Reports*, and they are his monument. These volumes contain two hundred and fifty-three of his opinions.

"He had the highest qualifications for the position of judge," says General Coburn.[64] "A sound judgment, an independent spirit, a clear perception, and a conscientious sense of his duty as judge. Patient and thorough in his investigation of cases, he was able to express in finished phrases his opinion of the merits of the controversy. No one could do this more directly or elegantly. His opinions are a fitting monument to his great ability as a judge."

> *"He had the highest qualifications for the position of judge," says General Coburn. "A sound judgment, an independent spirit, a clear perception, and a conscientious sense of his duty as judge."*

At the end of his second term, he was a victim of the politics of the day as we have described in the sketch of Judge Dewey. On retirement from the bench he resumed the practice at Madison; but in 1869 Governor Baker appointed him judge of the Criminal Court of Jefferson County; and in 1870

[63] Taylor, *Indiana Bench and Bar*, 39.
[64] Taylor, *Indiana Bench and Bar*, 30.

he was elected judge of that court, but died suddenly December 6th of that year. That was the very day on which he was to take the oath of office.

In politics Sullivan supported the Whigs and later the Republicans, though he was democratic in his views, favoring the common man as against the large corporations of his town. He walked midway between the two aggressive politicians of his city, Jesse D. Bright and John G. Marshall. In 1850 he opposed the election of William McKee Dunn to the Constitutional Convention on the ground that he was a corporation partisan. At the outbreak of the Civil War he aided Governor Morton materially in marshalling the State's resources.

Woolen wrote of Sullivan:

> During the nine years he sat upon the Supreme Bench, he graced and honored the place. His associates were Judges Blackford and Dewey, and it is saying only what is well known that at no time since the organization of the Court has it stood so high as when Blackford, Dewey and Sullivan were the judges. Those men were different in their mental make-up, but they were able.
>
> Sullivan was the ablest writer of the three, as may be seen in reading the reports of the court of that era. His opinions, as recorded by Blackford, are models of legal composition. There is a grace and perspicuity in his style but seldom found, and had he chosen to be a writer of legal books, he would, unquestionably have won a reputation even exceeding that which he earned on the bench.[65]

Judge Sullivan, Dewey and Blackford constituted the best court that sat under the old Constitution, if indeed it has been excelled in the history of the State.[66]

All were college trained men representing Williams, William and Mary, and Princeton, three leading colleges of that day. Each man was thoroughly devoted to the law. Each brought his own individual strength to the bench.

[65] Woolen, *Biographical and Historical Sketches of Indiana*, 360.
[66] Monks, *Courts and Lawyers of Indiana*, 209.

Blackford was learned in the law, diligent in searching out every precedent that could possibly throw light on the case at the bar. Dewey knew the law, but prepared also to rest all his decisions on the principles of morality and politics as well as precedent. Sullivan brought to the bench a catholicity of training and appreciation that gave his decisions a literary elegance not at all times common to the law. Literary elegance with Sullivan meant, an expression devoid of all temporary provincial or foreign terms, such an expression as would in plain English go to the point and there stop. Politics with Dewey meant the consideration of the final good of the State. Blackford would have excelled as a special pleader; Dewey, in a court of equity; Sullivan would have made an ideal trial Judge where the various interests of society came into active conflict. All made a team which for excellence was recognized not only in every State of the Union, but even in England.

Judge Sullivan was tall and commanding. In height he was over six feet, and his body was well proportioned. he had a good head and a good face. His hair was light and thin, unusually long, his eyes were dark brown, and his complexion was ruddy. His manner was dignified, and his carriage was good. He was always a gentleman; he was always polite. He was not an aggressive man, and did not have the influence his fellow townsmen, Marshall and Bright had; but he was a good citizen, and had the respect of all that knew him.

Of him Hon. Joseph McDonald said in a public address: "As a judge, he was learned and inflexible, and an ornament to the bench. As a practicing lawyer, he was able and honorable and an ornament to the profession. As a sincere Christian he was an ornament to the church. As a man of exalted personal character he was an ornament to society."

Judge Sullivan wrote two hundred and fifty-three opinions. His son Thomas L. Sullivan moved to the city of Indianapolis and was elected its Mayor by the Democrats: and his grandson Reginald, son of Thomas, was elected Mayor of that city on the Democratic ticket in November 1929 for a term of four years.

Image courtesy of Indiana Supreme Court.

Samuel E. Perkins

Judge Perkins was the only member of the Old Supreme Court that became a member of the New Court. In the Democratic Convention he defeated Isaac Blackford for the nomination as judge of the Third Judicial District in 1852. He served six years from January 3, 1853 to January 1859; and was reelected, serving until January 3, 1865. He was defeated at the October election 1864; but was elected again in October 1876, for a term beginning in January 1877, and served until his death December 17, 1879. He was born December 6, 1811, at Brattleboro, Vermont being the second son of John Trumbill and Catherine (Willard) Perkins. At an early age he became an orphan, and was adopted by William Baker, a farmer of Conway, Massachusetts, with whom he lived until he was twenty-one years old. The only schooling he had was three months annually in the local schools, and such as he obtained from self-instruction. After he attained his majority he taught school in the summer. The last year of his student life he spent at Yates County Academy, New York where he finished a fair classical education. He obtained his legal education in the office of Thomas J. Warren, and later in that of Henry Welles of Pan Yan, the county seat of Yates County. In 1836, alone he walked from Buffalo, New York to Richmond, Indiana. There, in the office of Judge J.W. Borden, he worked for his board during the winter of 1836-1837. In the spring he was admitted to the bar at Centerville, then the county seat of Wayne County; and opened an office at Richmond.

Perkins was a Democrat and the county was Whig. Richmond had a struggling Democratic paper, called the *Richmond Jeffersonian.* With this paper as a medium, Perkins set to work to build up an organization; he virtually became the editor of this paper and found recruits for his party among those disgruntled over the failure of the State canals. In 1839 and 1840 he again assumed control of this paper, and,

> *"It was because of his newspaper work that in after years he was said by the Republicans as not being a lawyer fit to sit on the Supreme Court Bench, but was only a newspaperman."*

because of his effective work, was appointed prosecuting attorney of the Sixth Judicial Circuit by Governor Whitcomb. In 1846 Governor Whitcomb appointed him judge of the Old Supreme Court, and his appointment was confirmed by the State Senate. It was because of his newspaper work that in later years he was said by the Republicans as not being a lawyer fit to sit on the Supreme Court Bench, but rather was only a newspaperman.

In 1857 he became a Professor of Law at Northwestern Christian University (now Butler University) and in 1870-1872 at Indiana University.

While on the bench he produced an *Indiana Digest* of eight hundred pages of the Supreme Court decisions. It covered the *Blackford Reports* and the first seven *Indiana Reports*. In 1859 he produced a work entitled "Indiana Practice." In 1868 he became editor of the *Indianapolis Herald*, a state Democratic organ.

Judge Perkins was a supporter of the principles of Jackson and Jefferson throughout his life. He did not believe in State prohibition; for he wrote the opinion in the Supreme Court that over threw the Prohibition Act of February 16, 1855.[67]

In 1838 he married Amanda Pyle, daughter of Joseph Pyle of Richmond. To them were born ten children. He never achieved the reputation as a lawyer, held by former members of the Supreme Court.

As a member of the Old Supreme Court he wrote two hundred and seventy-one opinions, which appear in the eighth *Blackford* and the first three *Indiana Reports.*

---

[67] Beebe v State 6 Ind 50.

Image courtesy of Indiana Supreme Court.

Thomas L. Smith

Judge Smith succeeded Judge Dewey and served from January 29, 1847 to January 3, 1853. It was a political appointment like that of Perkins as we have described in the sketch of Judge Dewey. He located at New Albany about 1839. He soon became deeply involved in politics, and his reputation was that of a politician rather than a lawyer or judge. The bar at New Albany was entirely Whig. About 1844 he was joined by Ashbel P. Willard, a Kentucky school teacher. The two soon built up a strong political organization ably supported by the *New Albany Ledger*, a new Democratic newspaper owned and edited by John Norman.

"Judge Smith was considered a good lawyer when he was appointed to the bench," says Oliver K. Smith.[68]

---

[68] Smith, *Early Indiana Trials*, 146.

He was possessed by nature, of a strong, clear, and vigorous intellect, well improved by reading. The Judge maintained a high reputation on the bench. Many of his decisions compare favorably, both in manner and legal accuracy, with those of his contemporaries. He delivered the opinion of the court in the great case of the State of Indiana, against the Vincennes University in error. The decision was afterwards reversed by the majority of the judges of the Supreme Court of the United States, but Chief Justice Taney, and the minority of the Court, concurred fully with the opinion of the Supreme Court of Indiana, pronounced by Judge Smith.

After leaving the bench he returned to the practice of law, and became counselor for the State Bank. His participation in the "bank frauds" at the opening of that bank deprived him of his reputation and position in the State.

He was reporter of one volume of *Indiana Reports*, now quite scarce, a private enterprise, published at New Albany in 1850. It is the smallest volume of any of the *Indiana Reports*, and contains only twenty-one opinions not found in *Blackford's* and *Indiana Reports*. According to the *Indiana Bench and Bar*:

He had practiced law but a few years before that time, [the date of his appointment in 1847] and had not a large practice. He had been a newspaper editor. At the State Convention of the Democrats before his nomination, he reported the platform and address of the Convention, which was said to have been written by him. These papers were composed in good style; and attracted a good deal of attention. He had no reputation beyond Floyd County and that region, as a lawyer, and his appointment was a surprise to the people without respect to party. He had applied for admission to the Supreme Court bar a few months before that time and failed in his examination, which was made in the form of written questions to be answered in a room into which all the applicants were obliged to remain until their written answers were prepared.[69]

---

[69]   Taylor, *Indiana Bench and Bar*, 40. Smith authored 209 options.

Chapter VII
The Reports

Judge Blackford prepared and edited eight volumes of reports of the opinions of the Old Supreme Court. They cover a period extending from the May 1817 Term to the November 1847 Term. They contain 4,399 pages of opinions and 349 pages of index.

From the very beginning these reports met with the favor of the bench and bar. Cases reported in them have been cited in every State in the Union, in the *United States Supreme Court Reports*, in a number of the United States District and Circuit Courts, in the Court of Claims and in the *Canadian Reports*.

Washington Irving said, when he was in England that citations were made to these *Reports* in the courts of that country.

Of Blackford's own opinions in the eight *Blackford's* and first three *Indiana Reports* 844 cases are cited. The total number of [Blackford's own] citations up to 1919 in other State Courts, in Federal Courts, and Canadian courts is 1,406. The Supreme Court of the United States has a number of times cited them. This is a fine tribute to Blackford's judicial ability.

Up to the year 1919 these *Reports* had been cited in other state courts opinions, in the United States court opinions and in the Canadian courts 3,417 times, an average of 427 per volume.

A very remarkable endorsement of their value, the soundness of the exposition of the law, and the confidence jurists of other states had in the discussions of the principles of the law that they contained. It may well be doubted if eight volumes of reports of any other state has been as often cited as these eight *Blackford Reports*.

In these eight volumes 1,649 cases are disposed of by written opinions, and 366 by mere memoranda, a total of 2,015, distributed as follows:

	Opinions	Memoranda
first *Blackford*	205	66
second *Blackford*	154	38
third *Blackford*	148	32
fourth *Blackford*	135	64
fifth *Blackford*	275	50
sixth *Blackford*	265	24
seventh *Blackford*	279	35
eighth *Blackford*	188	48
Total	1,649	366

The preface of the first volume is dated November 1830; and in it Blackford says, "This volume of Reports, containing decisions of the Supreme Court of the State during the first ten years of the Government is respectfully submitted to the Public." Thus the reports were three years behind with the Court opinions.

But not all the opinions rendered by the court are inserted in the *Blackford's*. In the preface it is said, "It was thought advisable to preserve this volume, as much as possible from anything that might be considered superfluous. With the approbation of the other members of the Court, therefore, some of the cases have been abbreviated and a few others, that have been overruled or were otherwise unimportant have been omitted." Perhaps some of the memoranda represent opinions that were abbreviated by Blackford.

Naturally the lawyers wanted to know what the cases were about that had been omitted and these omissions the publisher, Edwin A. Davis, of the second edition of the first *Blackford* undertook to supply. He says:

> This volume will be found to contain a number of cases omitted by Judge Blackford in his *Reports.* The late Gordon Tanner [reporter of the first *Indiana Report*] contemplated publishing a volume of the unreported cases, and a large subscription was obtained for the work. Taking as a basis of his calculations, the omitted cases embraced in the time covered by the first volume of the these *Reports,* Mr. Tanner was led to believe that these cases were much more numerous than they have proved to be. The records have been carefully searched and all the written opinions delivered by the Court from 1817 to 1847, omitted by Judge Blackford in his reports, will be found in this volume.

The number of opinions thus added to the first volume of *Blackford's Reports* in the second edition, including mere memoranda, is fifty-five; and they are printed at the end of the second edition of the first *Blackford.* Nowhere else is inserted in any of the second editions any additional cases. Presumably all cases omitted by Blackford have now been published.

How far Blackford took liberty with the original opinion in his revisions cannot be determined without a comparison with the original opinions in the Clerk's Office of the Supreme Court, a task not called for when such a careful judge as Blackford had made the revision.

Blackford added many notes to the opinions he edited that were in early days, and are yet, highly esteemed by the legal profession; and now some are as potent with the profession as the opinions themselves. In the second edition of these reports Mr. Edwin A. Davis added additional notes; but unfortunately he did not distinguish between his own notes and those of Blackford.

The syllabi are examples of fine reporting. They are written in concise and choice language. There is nothing superfluous about them, nothing obscure, nothing left to inference.

Blackford was an exceedingly careful reporter. His scholarship is manifest throughout the eight volumes. The contrast between the first editions and the second, both in type, paper, and binding is quite striking. In the first editions (now nearly disappeared), the paper, is excellent, the type clear, and the binding far superior to the Schirver binding of recent years.

The first, second and third *Indiana Reports* contain the opinions of the Old Supreme Court, none of the New Supreme Court, except three by Judge W.Z. Stuart, two by Davison and one by Addison L. Roache in volume three. Isaac Blackford, Samuel E. Perkins and Thomas L. Smith wrote all the opinions, with the exceptions just stated.

Blackford wrote 884 opinions that are printed in his eight volumes, three *Indiana* and *Smith Reports.* Holman wrote 138, Scott 97, McKinney 66, Dewey 384, Sullivan 256, Perkins 271, Smith 209 and Stevens 73, a total of 2,358. Besides these there appears in those eleven opinions 517 memoranda.

The first *Blackford* was published in 1830. It had 415 pages of opinions and 53 pages of index. In 1862, William A. Peele and Edwin A. Davis issued a second edition which was published by H.H. Dodd & Company of Indianapolis. At that time Peele was Secretary of State, but he had little time to devote to the work. At that time this first volume for years had been out of print, and hundreds of lawyers of the State were "unable to supply themselves with decisions which lie at the very foundations of the jurisprudence of the State," the editorial preface recites.

The second *Blackford* contains 486 pages of opinions and 33 pages of index. It was first published in 1834. It extends from the November 1826 Term to the May 1831 Term. The second edition was annotated by Warwick H. Ripley and published by Merrill, Hubbard, & Company in 1880.

The third *Blackford* contains 556 pages of opinions and 47 pages of index. It was published in 1836. It contains cases decided in May 1832 Term to end of November 1834 Term, The second edition was edited by Edwin A. Davis, and published by Merrill & Field in 1870.

The fourth *Blackford* has 556 pages of opinions and 47 pages of index. It covers from the November 1838 Term to May 1841 Term. The second edition was edited by Edwin A. Davis, and published by Merrill & Field in 1870.

The fifth *Blackford* has 605 pages of opinions and 40 pages of index. It covers the November 1838 Term to the May 1841 Term. The second edition was edited by Edwin A. Davis and published by Merrill & Field, 1870.

The sixth *Blackford* has 560 pages of opinions and 34 pages of index. It was published in 1846 by E.C. Chamberlain. It covers the November 1841 Term to November 1843 Term. Edwin A. Davis edited the second edition, published by Merrill & Field, 1870.

The seventh *Blackford* has 614 pages of opinions and 50 pages of index. It covers the November 1843 Term to November 1845 Term, inclusive. It was published in 1847. The second edition was annotated by Edwin A. Davis and published by Merrill & Field, 1870.

The eighth *Blackford* has 590 pages of opinions and 50 pages of index. It covers the May 1846 Term to the November 1847 Term. It was published in 1850. The second edition was annotated by Edwin A. Davis and published by Merrill & Fields, 1870.

There is no ninth *Blackford Report.*

Blackford had prepared in part a ninth volume before he went out of office. His eighth volume contained all the opinions filed at the November 1847 Term. In 1850 appeared Judge Stevens' report. At the time of its appearance Blackford was preparing a ninth volume. The appearance of Stevens' report was a surprise to Blackford; and was the only serious jar in his intercourse with any one of his colleagues. To him it was an offense of a slight nature, but there was no open outbreak. The fact was manifest that he was too slow in preparing and publishing his reports.

The Bar of the State was impatient with the tardiness in the reporting of the opinions of the Supreme Court. There was no West Publishing Company then publishing opinions four or five weeks after they were filed in the Clerk's office. The matter was discussed in the Constitutional Convention of 1850. Thus Henry P. Thornton of Floyd County, said, "It is well known that much inconvenience is frequently experienced by delay, in the publication of these decisions."[70]

Thus when the second *Blackford* was published in 1834 the last case reported had been decided at the May Term 1831. It was three years behind; the Third was two years behind; the Fourth, two years; the Fifth, three years; the Sixth, three years; the Seventh, two years; and the Eighth, three years. It was proposed to create the Office of Reporter by a provision in the Constitution. It was also proposed to make the Clerk of the Court the publisher of the opinions. A similar provision was discussed to make the Attorney General the reporter, which office was then under contemplation but which never matured in that body of delegates. There was decided opposition to a judge of the court being the reporter. "I am opposed, then," said delegate Thornton, "to the Supreme Court appointing their own reporter, and still more opposed to having a man directly elected by the people to fulfill the duties of such an officer. If we are to have such an office, I want to have a man who shall stand aloof from the Supreme Court."[71]

In the Convention dissatisfaction was expressed with reports of opinions that had hitherto been made. Reference has been made to the revision of the Court's opinions that Blackford had indulged in; and this fact drew fire. "I believe," said Delegate Thornton, "that hitherto it has been a matter of complaint that the reporters of the decisions of the Supreme Court have not been exactly what they should be, and, sir, although I do not mean to implicate a judge of that Court in any way, but I undertake to say

[70] *Debates of the Indiana Constitutional Convention,* Vol. 2, 1684.
[71] *Debates of the Indiana Constitutional Convention,* Vol. 2, 1661.

that opinions and decisions have been reported which have never been pronounced."[72]

And he continues:

> I cannot avoid referring here to one case in particular, which will be found in Third *Blackford*, the case of Parker versus Smith, a very important case in relation to tax titles. Although that decision was given at great length, and the strongest reasons assigned in support of it, there is in the reports a mere light note of it; and I have no doubt whatever, that it was owing to the interest which some gentlemen delving in tax titles that that decision was cut down and reduced almost to a nullity.[73]

The upshot of the question was that the Constitutional Convention did not create the office of Reporter or Attorney General, but provided that, "The General Assembly shall provide, by law, for the speedy publication of the decisions of the Supreme Court made under this constitution; but no judge shall be allowed to report such decisions."[74]

The first *Indiana* contains opinions only of the Old Supreme Court. Horace E. Carter was the Reporter, having been elected by the people in February, 1852. It covers the May 1847 Term to the November 1849 Term, inclusive. It was published in 1852, Austin H. Brown being the publisher. In his preface Carter says:

> This is the first volume of Report's under the new Constitution. The processes of the law creating the office [of Reporter] have been closely followed. All the written opinions delivered within the period over which the volume extends have been published in the manner in which they were delivered,

[72] *Debates of the Indiana Constitutional Convention*, Vol. 2, 1661.
[73] *Debates of the Indiana Constitutional Convention*, Vol. 2, 1661. The case of Parker v. Smith is reported in the fourth *Blackford* (page 70), and not in the third *Blackford*. It has a note appended to it by Judge Blackford that is longer than the opinion memorandum. It does not say who wrote the original opinion.
[74] Art. VII, Sec. 6. The Legislature since undertook to require that each judge of the Supreme Court prepare syllabi for the opinions he wrote; but the Court held the Statute unconstitutional. Ex Parte Griffiths, 118 Ind. 83; 20 N. 513.

and without any abridgement whatever. The plan of *Blackford's Reports* have been followed in every particular, in order that the profession might have a connected series.

It has 586 pages of opinions and 23 of index.

The second *Indiana* has 671 pages of opinions and 70 pages of index. It covers the May 1850 Term to May 1851 Term, inclusive. Horace E. Carter was the Reporter. W. W. Thornton annotated the second edition which has the imprint of Bower-Merrill Co., 1890 on the title page, but in the preface to the second edition John C. Shoemaker appears as the publisher. It contains opinions of only the Old Supreme Court.

The third *Indiana* has 585 pages of opinions and 59 pages of index. It covers the November 1851 Term and November 1852 Term, inclusive. Albert G. Porter is the Reporter; Warwick H. Ripley annotated the second edition; and the Bower-Merrill Co. published it in 1890, but Ripley signs his preface as of 1882. It concludes the opinions of the Old Supreme Court, but contains three by William Z. Stuart, two by Samuel E. Perkins, two by Andrew Davison, and two by Addison L. Roache, of the New Supreme Court, who were elected October 12, 1852, and took their seats January 3, 1853.

In the first *Indiana* appears 55 opinions of Blackford, 52 of Perkins, 58 of Smith, and 61 memoranda. In the second appears 80 of Blackford, 66 of Perkins and 63 of Smith, and 67 memoranda. In the third, 56 of Blackford, 76 of Perkins, 67 of Smith, and 11 memoranda. This makes a total of 573 opinions and 135 memoranda.

The first *Indiana* has been cited in other States and in the United States Courts 206 times, the second 306 times, and the third 270 times.

The opinions in the eight *Blackford's* require 4,399 pages and the syllabi 349.

A *Report of Opinions* was issued by Thomas L. Smith, one of the judges of the Court, as was heretofore stated, which was published in 1850 by Kent and Norman of New Albany. It was copyrighted by Smith. 152 cases in *Smith's Report* appear in the first *Indiana;* but it has 21 cases not published elsewhere. All the opinions it contains were rendered during the four terms of 1848 and 1849.

The first volume of *Blackford's Reports* on its publication at once took its place along side of the reports of Massachusetts and New York; and the succeeding volumes increased the popularity of the same. They were used and quoted far and wide. They are frequently cited by authors. Chancellor [James Kent?] declared they were "replete with extensive and accurate law learning, the notes of the learned reporter annexed to the cases being especially valuable"; and also said, "It is an interesting fact to find not only the *lex mercatoria* of the English equity system adopted and enforced in the State of Indiana as early as 1820, when we consider how recently the country had there arisen from a wilderness into a cultured and civilized community."

These notes were the forerunners of the modern method of annotating cases.

Appendixes

Appendix One
Blackford's Ancestry According To Thornton

Editors Note: This section originally appeared as a large, in-text citation within Thornton's manuscript. I have removed, reformatted, and placed it here for ease of reading.

I[Thornton] took this information from articles in the *Somerset County Historical Review* entitled "A Famous Western Jurist, Native of Somerset," written by G.A. Van Doren Honeyman, Plainfield, New Jersey.[1] My own view [Thornton's] of the New Jersey ancestry of Judge Blackford is as follows, subject to correction if any data can be found showing it erroneous:

Samuel Blackford, perhaps English born, certainly of English descent, was deeded by patent "in right of John Molleson," a lot of land in Middlesex County, N.J., north of Bound Brook, i.e. in Piscataway township on Aug. 16, 1695.[2] His wife's first name was Ann. By his will, probated April 29, 1712, he is known to have left sons Benjamin, Daniel, Samuel, and John, whose descendants for a time had large families of Blackfords, especially in Piscataway township and elsewhere.[3] Benjamin, Daniel and Joseph, apparently, were privates in the New Jersey Militia in the Revolutionary War (per the Newton military records); and both Benjamin and Daniel were long judges of Somerset, appointed in 1788.

[Samuel's son] Daniel, also of Piscataway, whose wife was Ruth, had sons Benjamin, Joseph, Samuel and Daniel. There were three sons named Daniel, the one to survive being born Sept. 29, 1720.[4]

Daniel of Bound Brook, wife perhaps Margaret, whose will, probated Oct. 14, 1778, named his sons Daniel and Joseph. Joseph was the father of Judge Blackford.[5]

---

[1] G. A. Van Doren Honeyman, "A Famous Western Jurist, Native of Somerset," *Somerset Historical Review* 5 (January 1916): 1-14.

[2] *East Jersey Deeds*, Book D, 203; (N.J. Archives, Vol. XXI, p. 227).

[3] *Trenton Unrecorded Wills*, Vol. 9, 67.

[4] *Piscataway Register of Births in N.J. Historical Proceedings*, Third Series, Vol. 2, 73-74.

[5] *Trenton Wills*, Book 20, 137.

Appendix Two
Condit Family Genealogy According To Thornton

Editors Note: This section originally appeared as a large, in-text citation within Thornton's manuscript. I have removed, reformatted, and placed it here for ease of reading.

Blackford's half-sister Charlotte Teressa married Daniel Dayton Condit, who was born in Hanover, Morris County, N.J., October 21, 1797, on February 3, 1827. Not long after this marriage they moved to Sullivan County, Indiana (about 1830), but changed their residence to Terre Haute. He was a wagonmaker, but later with his son John, engaged in mercantile business. He died in Terre Haute on January 21, 1877; his widow, Charlotte Teressa, died November 9, 1881. Their children were (1)John Dayton—born September 17, 1825, died March 31, 1900; (2)Isaac Blackford—born June 5, 1828, died October 8, 1828; (3)Blackford—born August 6, 1829, died March 27, 1903; (4)Mary Teressa—born November 10, 1835, died September 19, 1836; (5)Aaron Dayton—born March 17, 1843, died February 28, 1910.

Blackford Condit became a minister February 26, 1862. He [later] married Sarah Louisa Mills, the daughter of Professor Caleb Mills, the father of the Common School system of Indiana, and whose memory the city of Indianapolis has honored by naming its principal high school, "Caleb Mills High School." She died March 13, 1914. Rev. Condit graduated from Wabash College in 1854 and from Lane Theological Seminary in 1857. Of his eight children, three were surviving in January 1916; Allen Condit, a lawyer of Terre Haute; Helen, unmarried, of Terre Haute; and Joseph Dayton, a physician located in Pasadena, California.

For these data, as well as others, the writer is indebted to G.A. Van Doren Honeyman's article in the *Somerset County Historical Quarterly*, published in Somerville, New Jersey, 1916.[6] Mr. Honeyman made a very exhaustive research into the ancestors of Isaac Blackford and the descendants of his half-sister, Charlotte Teressa.

---

[6] Honeyman, "A Famous Western Jurist."